RETURN TO DUTY

RETURN TO DUTY

An Account of Brickbarns Farm, Merebrook and Wood Farm
U.S. Army hospitals in Malvern, Worcestershire 1943-45

Best wishes
Fran and *[signature]*

Fran & Martin Collins

BREWIN BOOKS

First published by
Brewin Books Ltd, 56 Alcester Road,
Studley, Warwickshire B80 7LG in 2010
www.brewinbooks.com

ISBN: 978-1-85858-454-6

A Cataloguing in Publication Record
for this title is available from the British Library.

Typeset in Plantin
Printed in Great Britain by
Cromwell Press Group

CONTENTS

INTRODUCTION

On 7th December 1941 the events at Pearl Harbour altered the position of the United States with regard to the war in Europe. Four days after congress had declared war on Japan, Germany and Italy declared war on the United States. America found itself involved in a war on two fronts; this resulted in plans being made to send troops both to the Pacific and to the European theatres of war.

It was decided that the U.S. authorities would make arrangements for the build up of U.S. troops in the U.K. which would serve as a staging area for the expected Allied invasion of Europe. Codenamed Operation Bolero, known to some as the 'Allied invasion of Britain', plans were put into motion for the billeting and living arrangements for the large numbers of U.S. service men who would be training in the U.K. prior to the invasion.

From the beginning the Medical Department were involved in these arrangements. It was necessary for the department to ensure that there was provision for the care of both wounded and ill soldiers. For the period prior to the invasion the army would require a garrison medical establishment to care for its sick and injured during the build up and waiting period as well as additional hospitals for Air Force casualties. After the commencement of the Cross Channel Assault extra hospitals would be required to accommodate the expected flow of casualties.

The responsibility for organising the hospital provision in the U.K. belonged largely to General Paul R. Hawley, the E.T.O. Chief Surgeon. He began by requisitioning a small number of established British hospitals, although the majority of these had already been set aside for British casualties. Hawley then required that the British War Office find sites for 35 station hospitals which were each to be less than five miles from each centre of concentration of U.S. troops in the U.K. The War Office and the Ministry of Agriculture then worked together to select suitable sites, usually in parks or estates to avoid building on farm land. By August 1942 33 sites had been located.

Hawley aimed to group the larger general hospitals in groups of four or five units for greater efficiency. He requested that the British find locations with adequate rail connections for hospital trains without disrupting overall traffic patterns. After consulting the railway authorities the War Office decided to place the first three centres in Cirencester, Great Malvern and Whitchurch (Shropshire) and in July 1942 it ordered the construction of fifteen general hospitals in groups of five at the three centres.

In Malvern construction was begun on five general hospitals, each having the capacity for 1084 beds. Two hospitals were to be built at Blackmore park (Plants 4172 and 4173) one at Brickbarns Farm (Plant 4174), one at Merebrook (Plant 4175) and one at Wood Farm (Plant 4176). The hospitals were to operate under the jurisdiction of the 12th Hospital Centre based in Malvern Link. Each would specialise in different types of surgery and treatment so that as patients arrived, usually by train, in Malvern, they could be sent to the hospital which would best deal with their needs.

Unfortunately, due to poor weather, lack of man power and lack of materials the U.S. hospital building programme in the U.K. fell behind schedule and it was necessary for Hawley to put back his timetable for the shipment of hospital units to the U.K. Even so the advance parties of the hospital units arriving in Malvern in the later part of 1943 and early parts of 1944 found British construction companies still working on site to complete the buildings. On some sites construction workers were even occupying the living quarters of the hospital personnel.

General Paul R. Hawley (U.S. Archives).

Colonel Lehman, Commanding Officer of 12th Hospital Centre at Malvern (The 53rd General Hospital Year Book).

The first U.S. hospital unit to arrive in Malvern was the 19th General Hospital in September 1943. This unit operated Blackmore Park Site One. The following month it was joined by the 65th General Hospital at Blackmore Park Site Two. In November the 56th General Hospital arrived at Brickbarns Farm to find that they were to run a neuropsychiatric hospital until the 96th General Hospital arrived in January 1944. The hospital at Brickbarns Farm was to be the only Neuropsychiatric General Hospital in

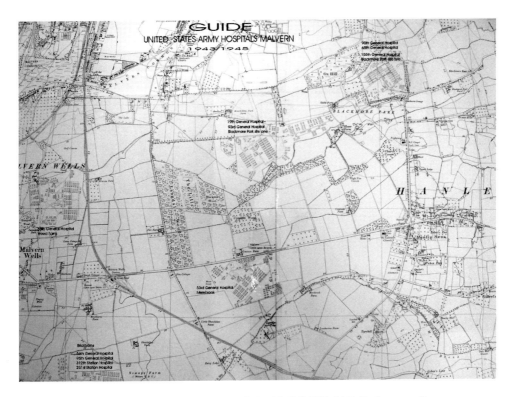

Reproduction of 1954 SO831424 and 1955 SO772417 Ordnance Survey map showing hospital sites (With the kind permission of Ordnance Survey).

Europe until the 130th General Hospital N.P. was established in Belgium towards the end of 1944. For the majority of its patients this hospital was essentially a holding hospital or Z.I. (Zone of the Interior) hospital caring for neuropsychiatric patients that could not be returned to duty, whilst they awaited transport back to the States. This hospital site was later occupied by the 312th station hospital which was followed by the 53rd General Hospital. At the end of the war it was home to the 123rd Station Hospital.

In March 1944 the 53rd General Hospital arrived at Merebrook. This hospital specialised in burns and plastic surgery and also functioned as a Z.I. hospital, particularly towards the end of the war when many of its patients were soldiers who had been too badly wounded to be returned to duty. Also in March 1944 the 55th General Hospital, whose specialism was in neural surgery, arrived at Wood Farm.

The joint aim of the five hospitals in the Malvern area was to return as many patients to duty as possible. In the period after D-Day even the 96th General

Hospital sent a percentage of its patients back into service. It was not appropriate to send all of the patients back to combat situations so many were reassigned to non-combatant units such as postal or quartermaster units.

This book sets out the history of the three hospital sites at Brickbarns Farm, Merebrook and Wood Farm respectively. It looks at the experiences of the staff and their patients through eyewitness accounts and the impact of the hospital on the surrounding area and its inhabitants.

Wounded patients from Malvern hospitals being evacuated by train at Malvern Wells Station (R. Rotundo).

Part One:

Brickbarns Farm – Plant 4174

Chapter 1

56TH GENERAL HOSPITAL

Plant 4174 at Brickbarns Farm opened as a hospital site on 10 November 1943. The first hospital unit to occupy the site was the 56th General Hospital.

The 56th General Hospital had been originally formed during the First World War at Camp Greenleaf, Georgia as Base Hospital Number 56. It sailed from the U.S. in August 1918 and arrived in France on 13 September. It took station at Allerey (Saone-et-Loire) where it remained until 1 February 1919. The unit then became inactive until it was reactivated at Fort Jackson, South Carolina on 1 February 1941 under the command of Lieutenant Colonel Daniel J. Sheeton.

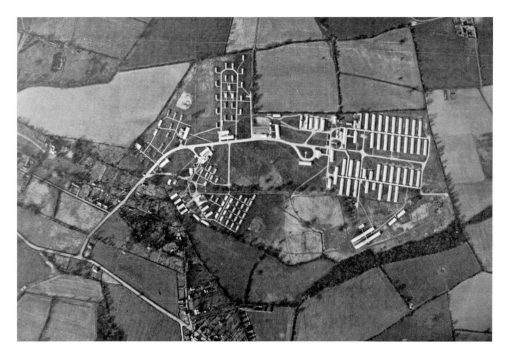

Aerial view of Brickbarns hospital site (English Heritage).

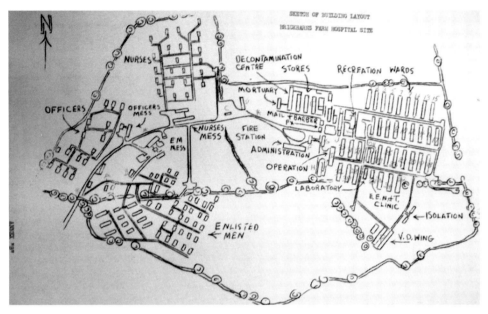

Plan of Brickbarns site (56th General Hospital Archives).

On 13 July 1943 the 56th General Hospital was alerted for departure. The personnel were ready to move out on 12 August but spent the day waiting for a train which did not arrive until 0100 hours the next morning. The unit arrived at Camp Shanks, New York at 0330 hours the following morning in a torrential rainstorm. The 56th spent the next three days preparing for departure overseas but then were taken off alert and moved to Fort Devens, Massachusetts on 24 August 1943. While at Camp Shanks five Red Cross workers reported for duty. They accompanied the unit to Fort Devens but here two girls were relieved from duty and replaced by two others. The transfers were made:

" ... *as a means towards better harmony in the Red Cross Group" (56th General Hospital Archives).*

Finally on 8 October the 56th embarked from the Boston Port of Embarkation. From here the group sailed to Liverpool, England aboard HMS 380, arriving on October 17 1943 and disembarking the following day.

The Chief Nurse describes the nurses' debarkation:

"One hundred bewildered nurses neatly dressed in class A uniform but loaded down with gas mask, musette bag, pistol belt and handbag stumbled down the gang plank, stepped out on foreign soil and said, almost in unison, 'What Now?'" (56th General Hospital Archives).

From Liverpool the unit travelled by train to Malvern. The Chief Nurse records that the train had six person compartments but no heat. The personnel arrived cold and hungry at Malvern Wells Station where they were met by the advance party which had arrived on October 6, and taken to Brickbarns where they were given a hot meal. The nurses were then assigned to nissen huts alphabetically, seven to a hut.

When the personnel awoke the next morning they were pleasantly surprised. The archivist describes the hospital as being:

Insignia of the 56th General Hospital. Design approved 15.01.1942. The cross formed by the square with chamfered corners represents the unit's medical mission. The unit was originally organised at Camp Green Leaf, Georgia in 1918 with initial service in France in World War I, shown by the fleur de lis. (Authors' collection).

" ... *Ideally located on the slope of one of the highest hills in Great Britain, which on clear days, provides a magnificent view to the summit and further down into the valley. ... As the name of the location implies the hospital has been constructed on a farm site and much of the surrounding countryside is still devoted to agriculture. In one instance cattle and sheep can be seen grazing within 100 feet of the nurses' quarters. ... The surrounding community is suburban and a sparsely settled residential section approaches as far as the gates*" *(56th General Hospital Archives)*.

The personnel spent the first month at the site preparing for the arrival of the first patients. The archives state that:

"The amount of carpentry, plumbing, electrical work, bricklaying and general repairing for maintenance alone is far beyond anything anticipated prior to employment. When this is added to the big job in this field of activity that is required initially for the opening of the hospital it easily assumes a major role in importance" *(56th General Hospital Archives)*.

Administrative and housing details were assigned and the enlisted men attended classes on geographical orientation and the European Theatre Policy regarding Negro troops. The latter being because of the lack of segregation in the U.K.

The nurses were required to make equipment such as surgery drapes and masks. They also cut out and folded gauze for dressings, washed and made beds, sorted equipment and rosters. One of the nurses recalls:

"We ran into difficulty in classifying some of the British material which we had to use – for weeks we used the pretty gay coloured squares sent to us for bedside tables, until we discovered they were the English version of bedpan covers" (56th General Hospital Archives).

Malvern Wells Train Station (96th General Hospital Year Book).

Officers area 56th General Hospital (96th General Hospital Year Book).

All of the personnel were expected to practise drill regularly. The Chief Nurse commented that:

"Drilling was not very satisfactory as high grass and mud and the variety of uniforms due to time limit, made us look anything but soldierly as we marched, however we drilled as ordered. We practised gas mask drill until we could almost put the masks on backwards" (56th General Hospital Archives).

In the first few weeks contact was made with organisations in the Malvern area to create opportunities for social activities with nearby British units. Officers, nurses and enlisted men were also invited into the homes of neighbouring British families. Contact was also made with Special Service agencies and requisitions placed for radios, furniture and games to equip the recreation rooms.

On arrival at Brickbarns a ward had been put aside to use as a recreation room but it was necessary to vacate this when the hospital opened to patients. It was decided to combine the officers and nurses mess into one building so that the nurses dining hall could be converted to a recreation room and club for officer personnel.

The unit was fortunate enough to have its own orchestra. Prior to the movement overseas to Britain a search for musical talent in the command had been made and the 56th General Hospital Orchestra composed. During the 56th's time at Brickbarns the orchestra was in demand to provide music for dances for the personnel and patients and also for playing at the other hospitals in the locality.

Cook stoves in Enlisted men's Mess. (56th General Hospital Archives).

Shortly after their arrival at Brickbarns the personnel of the 56th were surprised to be informed that their unit was to temporarily operate a neuropsychiatric hospital of 674 capacity at Brickbarns whilst also opening and operating a 834 bed station hospital 60 miles away at Tyntesfield Park, Flax Bourton, Somerset.

As the troop strength in the E.T.O. increased there was seen to be a definite need for facilities for neuropsychiatric patients. Facilities were required for diagnosis and treatment of treatable cases, neuropsychiatric screening of combat units pre-invasion and the care and treatment of non-curable psychiatric disorders.

To provide for the needs of neuropsychiatric patients in the European Theatre of Operations 12,000 to 15,000 beds were set up in neuropsychiatric sections of approximately 150 general hospitals. It was also necessary to establish three specialist neuropsychiatric units which could provide more definitive therapy. The specialist establishments would have the facilities to physically separate psychotics and other 'nonsalvable' cases from those that could be treated.

The 312th Station Hospital, known as the 'Neurosis Centre' was to provide definitive therapy for the less serious cases where there was a chance that the patients may be returned to duty in the E.T.O., albeit in a non-combat unit.

The 36th Station and the 56th General (later to be replaced by the 96th General) Hospitals were to function as diagnostic and therapeutic centres for the more serious psychiatric cases. The 36th Station Hospital, based in Exeter, was the first N.P. hospital to be set up in the E.T.O. It incorporated a school of neuropsychiatry which provided refresher courses for the younger psychiatrists in the theatre as well as a training centre for medical officers not previously trained in psychiatry.

It was only by chance that the 56th was selected to be a N.P. hospital. Once the specialised Tables of Organisation and Equipment for N.P. hospitals had been approved in October 1943 it was decided that the next non-affiliated general hospital to arrive in the U.K. would be altered accordingly. The 56th happened to be that hospital.

It was decided that Detachment A, comprising 25 officers, 25 nurses, a hospital dietician, a physiotherapy aide and 200 enlisted men, would be assigned to run the station hospital in Somerset but because Detachment A was considered to be a provisional unit it was not authorised any extra T/E equipment. It was necessary to split the supplies and available vehicles between the two destinations which:

" ... *caused a considerable amount of inconvenience in transportation difficulties*" (*56th Archives*).

It was necessary to maintain a constant liaison between the two sites and this involved much transportation of personnel and equipment. Additional officers, nurses and enlisted men were sent to join Detachment A as the need arose. The nurses were rotated between the two hospitals. By the end of 1943 28 officers, 29 nurses, a physiotherapy aide, a hospital dietician and 212 enlisted men were serving at Tyntesfield Park. Fortunately, because

Motor Pool at Tyntesfield Hospital (56th General Hospital Archives).

both hospitals were only operating at about one third capacity the situation was manageable.

Once Detachment A had left Brickbarns the main unit embarked on an intensive psychiatric training programme. At this point the 56th had only two qualified psychiatrists, the Chief of the Medical Service and the Chief of Neuropsychiatry, Major Paul N. Lemka. Together they launched a training programme in neuropsychiatry for ward officers so that by the time the first patients arrived in November all physicians had a basic understanding of neuropsychiatry. The personnel were keen to learn and:

"The net result of such enthusiasm and individual effort was the satisfactory care of this type of patient and a new respect for the necessity of every physician having at least a basic understanding of neuropsychiatry" (56th General Hospital Archives).

Because the hospital had been built to serve the needs of a normal general hospital some adaptations had to be made for its use as a N.P. hospital. It was necessary for the ward layout to be adapted to provide for the reception of disturbed and semi disturbed cases. The 56th made adaptations to change some of the wards to 'closed type' wards:

"Windows were barred with wooden frames covered with gauge wire from floor to ceiling. Four cells of brick construction, with solid wood doors and steel and wire stove protectors were added on each ward. Special ceiling lights were installed and minor changes in plumbing fixtures were made" (56th General Hospital Archives).
Even when this was completed security remained a problem. The Chief Nurse reported that:

Closed Ward (56th General Hospital Archives).

"Only too often a patient would smash a door or crawl through a window" (*56th General Hospital Archives*).

One patient escaped through the window on his ward and then got back into the ward by picking all the locks that barred his way. The archives state that:

"Much damage to buildings was occasioned by disturbed patients kicking through doors, smashing windows, breaking ceiling lights with thrown objects, and other occurrences of like nature. This was almost a continuous process" (*56th General Hospital Archives*).

Other minor adaptations were made to the buildings; sinks and benches were moved to better positions, shelving was constructed and extra doorways made. It was decided to use the large Venereal Disease ward for the storage of quartermaster supplies and some buildings were adapted to provide adequate office space.

The one facility which caused the most problems on the hospital site was the heating. The Chief Nurse reported that:

"The weather was always cold and damp and after calisthenics and drill each morning your leggings and fatigues would be soaked. The big problem here ... was to keep warm. ... It took a plan where one person got up every two hours to add fuel to keep a fire going" (*56th General Hospital Archives*).

Each ward would have seven stoves to keep stoked, smaller rooms had less. A total of 400 stoves were spread over the hospital site. The archivist for the 56th records:

"To keep the stoves supplied with fuel, stoked and policed, was undoubtedly one of the largest single claims on manpower in the unit" (56th General Hospital Archives).

The unit had the use of 15 civilian workers on site, some of whom helped with maintaining the stoves. Others worked as typists, telephone operators, cleaners, labourers and maintenance personnel. By employing civilians

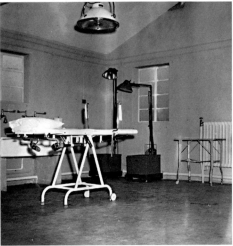
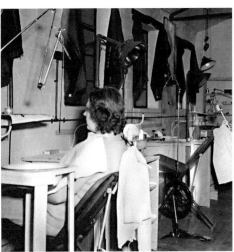

Interiors of buildings on Brickbarns site showing adaptations and furniture made by utility section of 56th General Hospital. Top left and bottom left: Laboratories. Top right: Operating theatre. Bottom right: Dental clinic. (Photographs supplied on this page are from the 56th General Hospital Archives).

 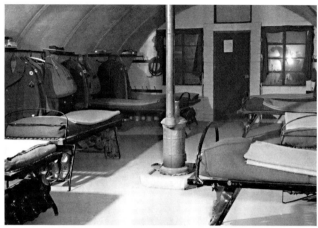

Top left: Autoclaves (56th General Hospital Archives). Top right: Interior of Enlisted men's hut showing stove in centre (56th General Hospital Archives).

military personnel could be released for other duties. Unfortunately the 56th was not satisfied with the work of the civilian clerical personnel and telephone operators. The archivist reports:

"Just as it takes many months to develop an enlisted man into a really proficient army clerk, so it will be before civilian typists will be adequately trained for this type of duty, especially in view of prior training in methods different from those in use by the United States Army. It was found that enlisted men with only a few weeks training were more efficient, conscientious and reliable operators than civilian personnel" (56th General Hospital Archives).

On 10 November 1943 the 56th General Hospital was officially opened for the reception of patients as a 674 bed general hospital (NP), later to be raised to a 1025 bed capacity. Shortly after this it received its first contingent of patients. In the main patients came from units that were training in the U.K. while awaiting the expected invasion of the continent. The mission of the hospital was to diagnose the psychiatric disorders of soldiers whose mental illness made them unfit for military service and then keep them hospitalised until the necessary arrangements could be made to ship them home.

Carlton Hunt, a doctor with the 56th comments that:

"Despite these serious mental problems patients were sometimes expected to line up for inspections and stand at the foot of their beds. Making them comply was not an easy task. This bizarre procedure made me wonder who was crazier, the patients or our commanding officer." (The History of Neuroscience in Autobiography – Larry R. Squire).

A large contingent of the patients arriving at the 56th was transferred back to the United States to complete their treatment or be discharged from the service. The hospital completed three relatively large evacuations from hospital to ship; patients were accompanied on the train journey by sufficient hospital personnel to ensure their safety and well being. A number of outpatients were also treated at the hospital.

The hospital operated in this capacity until January 1944 when the 56th General Hospital left Brickbarns and the remaining 211 patients in the installation were transferred to the 96th General Hospital, the incoming hospital unit.

During the short period of the 56th's operation at Brickbarns Farm 347 patients had been admitted of which 76 were transferred back to duty. Ten were transferred to other hospitals and 77 were evacuated to the United States, 25 surgical operations had also been carried out.

The archivist for the 56th sums up their time at Brickbarns:

"Although difficulties were encountered the adaptability and high spirit of cooperation displayed by the officers, nurses and enlisted men precluded any reverse of major import and the period of operation at this hospital closed uneventfully when the installation was turned over to the 96th General Hospital on 12 January 1944" (*56th General Hospital Archives*).

Headquarters 56th General Hospital was opened at 0001 hours 13 January 1944 at Tyntesfield Park Hospital site at which point Detachment A was absorbed by the parent unit.

Chapter 2

96TH GENERAL HOSPITAL (N.P.)

T he 96th General Hospital had been formed in 1942 at Camp Devens, Massachusetts. From here it moved to Camp Maxey, Paris, Texas, where it functioned as a regular general hospital under the command of Colonel Gambrell. He was succeeded by Lieutenant Colonel McKeen Caton who was in turn succeeded by Lieutenant Colonel Emmet M. Smith. On December 15 1943 the unit moved to the staging camp at Camp Kilmer, New Jersey where it remained until December 28. On December 28 the unit boarded the S.S. Dominion Monarch which sailed as part of a large convoy of vessels including the battleship Texas and seventeen destroyers.

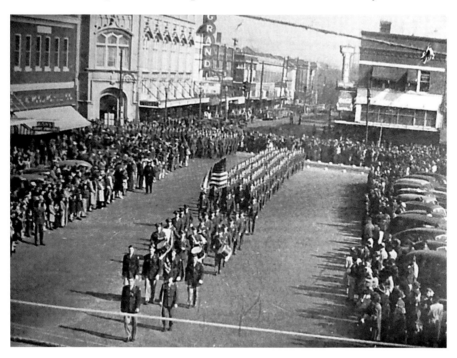

96th General Hospital on parade in Paris, Texas.
(96th General Hospital Year Book).

Left: H.M.S. Dominion Monarch. Right: Lieutenant Colonel Emmet M. Smith, Commanding Officer of the 96th General Hospital.

The convoy headed for Great Britain and after an uneventful voyage docked in Liverpool on the evening of 9 January 1944. The personnel debarked early the next morning and were transported by train to Malvern Wells, arriving at 3p.m.

The first three days at Brickbarns were spent in orientation so that on 13 January 1944 the unit was ready to take over the responsibilities and the care of the 211 patients under the jurisdiction of the 56th General Hospital. Like the 56th the 96th they had been unaware that they were to run a neuropsychiatric hospital until they arrived at Brickbarns. The orders for 11 January 1944 made the hospital:

Left: Signpost showing direction to 96th General Hospital. Middle: Personnel from the 96th General Hospital. Right: Entrance to the 96th General Hospital. (Photographs supplied on this page are from the 96th General Hospital Year Book).

" … largely responsible for the ultimate care and disposition of the psychotic patients in the European Theater of Operations" (96th General Hospital Archives).

The orders also rendered the hospital:

" … available for receiving any patients affected with any neuropsychiatric disease or disabilities if it is determined that the patient is not capable of rehabilitation to the end that he may be returned to duty status. Hence most of the dispositions from the organisation are necessarily to the Zone of the Interior" (96th General Hospital Archives).

Upon hearing the news that the 96th was to be a N.P. hospital a number of the personnel requested transfers. 15 officers were submitted for reassignment (eventually they were replaced by qualified psychiatrists). Lieutenant Colonel Smith had the unenviable task of reorganising and training existing hospital personnel to function as an N.P. hospital. The situation was further complicated by the sudden influx of a large group of patients in January quadrupling the original patient numbers. To cause added strain to the 96th, in the first couple of months it was subjected to a series of inspections. This was possibly because of its uniqueness in being the only N.P. hospital in the E.T.O. In one 20 day period the hospital was visited by 18 inspecting officers, including Major General Paul R. Hawley, the Chief Surgeon in the E.T.O.

Personnel specialising in psychiatric treatment from the 36th Station Hospital were transferred to the 96th to make up the staffing numbers and arrangements were made for additional medical officers specialising in neuropsychiatry to be assigned to the 96th. By April 1 the hospital was still ten officers under strength and it was not until September that the full quota of psychiatrists was present.

Originally Major Hugh Kiene was the only qualified psychiatrist on the staff. He was appointed chief of Psychiatric Service and organised training for the nurses, Red Cross workers, enlisted men and doctors who elected to remain with the 96th.

To fit in with the Table of Organisation for N.P. hospitals it was necessary to transfer out 26 of the 100 nurses originally assigned to the 96th. Of the remaining nurses only one had taken a neuropsychiatric Post Graduate Course while three had had three months affiliation in neuropsychiatric nursing while in training. An intensive course in neuropsychiatric nursing at the hospital was commenced straight away. A system was

Major Hugh Kiene (96th General Hospital Year Book).

Nurses at 96th General Hospital L-R 1st Lt. Anne La Monica,
1st Lt. Rita Hacker, 1st Lt. Sara Gray (96th General Hospital Year Book).
Below: Letter sent by nurse, Lt. Hacker (Authors' collection).

put into place whereby all nurses were rotated through the sections of the hospital so that all would become familiar with the function of management peculiar to each section.

Colonel Smith divided the hospital into three sections: Admissions, Treatment and Disposition. The Admissions Section consisted of wards 12 to 17 and held patients for around 5 days while their history was collated and physical examinations completed. If the patient needed treatment he was sent to the Treatment Section which comprised wards 1 to 3 and 5 to 11. Patients usually spent around fifteen days in this section.

Within the Treatment Section patients were segregated into particular wards according to the type of therapy or care needed. At the beginning treatment consisted of only emergency measures for the handling of disturbed patients like sedation and physical restraint. Treatment was gradually expanded to include shock therapy, insulin coma, individual and group psychotherapy, hypnosis and narcoanalysis.

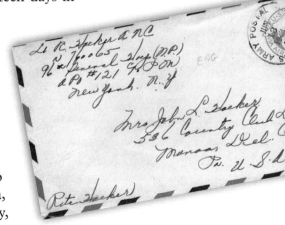

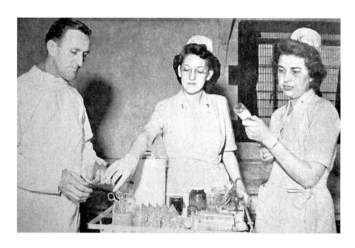

Sergeant Craner, Lt. Keefer and Lt. Hacker preparing for insulin treatment.
(96th General Hospital Year Book).

Major Walter Goldfarb was assigned to the Treatment Section when he joined the personnel in February 1944. He supervised the physical therapy methods which included electric shock and insulin coma treatment. On 15 February the first patient was treated with electric shock.

One of the patients given electric shock treatment was H. E. Harvey. He had been serving with the 8th Army Air Force since October 1943 and was admitted to hospital for nasal congestion in May 1944. While in hospital he was diagnosed as a neuropsychiatric patient and it was decided that he needed shock treatment. He remembers that many of the other patients kicked and fought the corpsmen who accompanied them to the treatment room whilst he remembers walking calmly.

He recalls one occasion when he became unconscious while undertaking the treatment and he remembers waking, terrified to see a large medic leaning over him in the act of giving him C.P.R. This image has always stayed with him.

When the patient's treatment was completed, or if he did not require treatment he was assigned to the Disposition section under the supervision of Major Paul Parker. This section was comprised of wards 18 to 31 and 33 to 35. It held patients for varying lengths of time depending on the facilities for evacuation back to the U.S.

Major Walter Goldfarb (96th General Hospital Year Book).

Left: Electric Shock equipment. Right: Major William Needles
(96th General Hospital Year Book).

Towards the end of the year the ward system was adapted as it was found that it was better for a patient to remain under the care of the same doctor from the time that he entered the hospital until he left. Doctors were assigned in pairs to supervise both an open and closed ward. It would then be possible to transfer a patient from an open to a closed ward and vice versa as necessary and still remain under the care of the same doctor. While the treatment wards were still used for the physical methods of treatment the patient returned to his own ward on the completion of the treatment.

19 of the 30 bed wards at Brickbarns were designated as 'closed wards' thus catering for 570 patients. As the term indicates these patients were confined to their wards. 14 wards were designated as 'open wards' allowing for 420 patients. There were 2 V.D. wards, each having 36 beds and two isolation wards with 10 beds in each. Ward 14 was kept for female patients (all female psychotic patients were treated at the 96th), wards 2 and 10 were kept for officers and ward 15 for prisoners. Ward 32 was used for medical and surgical patients from the personnel of the 96th.

As the hospital was not purpose built the 96th found, as the 56th had before them, that security was an issue, particularly on the closed wards. In his report for April to September 1944 Colonel Smith, who had been promoted by this time, reports that:

Major Paul Parker
(96th General
Hospital Year Book).

View of the wards (96th General Hospital Year Book).

"The wards are far from adequate in their construction for the care of the mentally disturbed patients. There were far too many hazards in the form of pipe projections etc. for the suicidally inclined patient. The wire netting at the windows was so meagrely secured that a patient could, with very little exertion, escape. It was not unusual for a disturbed patient to remove a bit of wall or roof when so inclined. The wooden slats of the latrine seat could easily be detached and used as an offensive weapon. The same held true for the bricks in the flimsily constructed partition in the latrine" (96th General Hospital Archives).

A number of the patients did 'escape' and local Malvern people remember seeing men wandering about in their dressing gowns in the area around the hospital. Godfrey Williams remembers:

"There was a large pool on the farm and it was not uncommon to see a disturbed American soldier standing in the pool pleading, 'Take me home, I want to go home.' They had no shoes or boots on their feet and were dressed only in ward clothes. My father and the others used to do their best to calm them down. On rare occasions there were more serious happenings when some of the patients used to climb up the mains electricity pylons and were found dead underneath them."

Richard Lloyd also remembers the patients being killed by the electricity pylons. He recalls a patient arriving at Danemoor Farm in pyjamas with no shoes. His family took the man into the farmhouse where they gave him a cup of tea and talked to him about farming while they waited for him to be picked up and taken back to the hospital.

Unlike the regular general hospitals whose remit was to return the patient to duty whenever possible the remit of the neuropsychiatric hospital was to treat patients so that they became less disturbed and calmer with a more positive outlook. It was hoped that most, when they reached the U.S., would be able to perform a positive role in civilian life. Only in a small number of cases was it expected that the patient's situation could be improved enough so that he could return to duty.

Colonel Smith writes in the archives for the 96th:

"Emphasis on patients returned to duty as practised in neuropsychiatric institutions further forward in the echelon of evacuation had to be replaced at the 96th ... by stressing the importance of the patient's mental condition. A feeling of defeat, failure and hopelessness existed in many patients on admission as they had been exposed to particularly traumatizing nicknames when their mental condition was such that they would not improve sufficiently to return to duty in the European Theatre of Operation. ... An attitude towards improvement in the patient's condition was important in order to maintain a good professional spirit and stimulate interest on the part of the medical officers. ... Our mission as psychiatrists, the obligation towards men who had been crushed by the juggernauts of war, and consideration for the civilian community to which these men would return seemed to compel the adaptation of such a policy" (96th General Hospital Archives).

Patient turnover at the 96th was rapid and the average stay was short. A large number of the patients had already been hospitalised for a number of

Patients returning home from the 96th (96th General Hospital Year Book).

HEADQUAR. S, 96TH(US) GENERAL HOSPITAL (. ,
V HOSPITAL GROUP (PROV)
APO # 121, U.S. ARMY

MEMORANDUM: 10 December 1944

TO   : Patients, 96th (US) General Hospital (NP).

A great many of you have passed thru several hospitals before arriving
here, have had to answer the same questions, and go through the same set of examinations repeatedly. This is unavoidable under present conditions but, at the
same time, tiresome and often confusing to the individual concerned. This memorandum is intended to clear up some of the confusion by telling you something
about the 96th General Hospital (NP) -- why you were sent here, what we attempt
to do here, what you are expected to do here, where you go from here.

The 96th General Hospital is equipped to take care of those men whose
problems could not be dealt with adequately in hospitals further forward in the
echelon, because either of lack of time or space, or the nature of the problem
involved. This hospital has special facilities to take care of the sort of difficulties that you are troubled by.

The medical officers have had years of experience in this field of
medicine, Psychiatry. You will be assigned to the ward of one of them, who will
as a rule have you under his care during your entire stay in this hospital. He
will go over you story patiently, try to find out how your difficulties arose,
and decide what should be done about them.

Psychiatrists know much more about conditions such as yours than they
did in the last war. They are able to detect signs that all is not well with a
man much sooner than was formerly the case, and to recommend the necessary treatment. For these reasons the outlook is much more hopeful than it used to be.
Because you happen to have heard of a veteran of the last war who was "nervous"
and has not recovered is no reason to take a hopeless attitude about yourself,
as some do.

For certain conditions there are special forms of treatment, of the
latest type, fully provided for in this hospital.

Another point to remember is that, as psychiatrists, our aim is to get
a man well -- as completely as possible and as quickly as possible -- whether
he is to return to duty in the army or to civilian life. We assume that the
man will want to carry on in whatever capacity he is most suited, in order to
win the war, and we look upon our job as that of rendering him as fit as possible
for that purpose, wherever he may be placed.

To what extent you improve and how quickly depends not only on the
medical officer, no matter how good he may be; it depends at least as much on
you, on your willingness to cooperate and to meet him half way, on your attitude.
Modern warfare puts strains and hardships on a man such as he has never run up
against before. It is no disgrace for a man to become upset or shaken under
such circumstances. But you must bear in mind that this upset is only a temporary affair. There is no reason why you should not, by your efforts and with
the help of the medical officer, get over you condition and be your old self
again.

You will find while you are here that an effort is made to keep every
man as busy as possible. This is done because it is an important part of treatment. The more a man does, the more quickly he proves to himself that he can

Appendix # 10   (1)

21

accomplish things and th sooner he gets back some of the elf confidence he
has lost. Being active, no matter how unimportant the job may seem, is better
than sitting around on a ward moping about yourself and letting your muscles
get flabby. We aim, therefore, at making the Rehabilitation Section as active
as possible by the participation in it of all patients capable of any type of
work or exercise.

The Red Cross is set up to assist in the recreational program, to provide certain types of occupational therapy, as well as to follow thru in certain
personal problems that a man may have, such as failure to hear from home in a
reasonable time, inability to contact his family, etc. Your ward officer will
refer you to the Red Cross when the indication arises.

As a soldier you will be expected to observe the usual rules and regulations. There is a reason for each of them. No large establishment can be run
with everyone doing exactly as he pleases.

When you have been in the hospital for a sufficiently long time for the
medical officer to study your condition and observe the progress you have made,
you will appear before a Medical Disposition Board. This board will discuss
the situation with you and determine, on the basis of all the facts, just
where you best fit in at the time. You will have the opportunity to assist the
board in its decision by telling the members of it just how you fell and whatever else you think has a bearing on the decision to be arrived at.

We think this hospital has a great deal to offer you toward getting
well -- provided that you feel the fight to regain your health is one worth
making and you are anxious to cooperate.

E.M. SMITH,
Colonel, M.C.,
Commanding Officer

Letter given out to patients on their arrival at the hospital
(96th General Hospital Archives).

months before they reached Brickbarns. Some of the patients had been assigned
to a limited duty assignment after treatment on N.P. wards in other general
hospitals but they had been unable to carry out their duties satisfactorily. Many
of the patients arriving at the 96th had already been put before the board which
decided whether they would be sent back to the Zone of the Interior and were
merely biding their time while awaiting their passage home. Many displayed
confusion and bewilderment on arrival at yet another hospital. To counteract
this, the hospital produced a memorandum to be distributed to each patient on
admission. It attempted to explain the reason for the patient's admission, their
position in the hospital and their probable disposition.

The officers at the 96th felt that it was important to treat the patients with
care and consideration and in a positive manner. In one of his training
lectures at the 96th Major William Needles was to tell his students:

"Patients are sick people until unless proved otherwise. Their querulousness, truculence, obscenity, assaultiveness must be viewed objectively and without resentment, not to be dismissed as 'nutty', 'batty', 'cracked'. Patients respond to a friendly attitude" (96th General Hospital Archives).

After D-Day the patient intake changed. Some patients were admitted who, after treatment, would be able to return to duty in the army, albeit in a non-combatant unit. At this point Colonel Smith describes the programme as being:

" ... long range in scope and specifically pointing towards either making the patient a better soldier in the United States Army, or a more useful, socially productive citizen upon return to civilian life" (96th General Hospital Archives).

Overall, almost two thirds of the patients received by the 96th were not psychotic. About 4% of the admissions were neurological cases and at the beginning of June 1944 a 60 bed ward was set aside for neurological patients.

The archivist notes that:

"While this ward was separated as a distinctly neurological ward the patients had considerable esprit and a feeling of satisfaction, justifiable or not, in being distinguished from the larger group of psychotic patients" (96th General Hospital Archives).

With the large influx of patients following D-Day it was necessary to utilise all available beds and psychiatric patients were admitted to the Neurological ward. It was noted that morale in the ward deteriorated rapidly after this.

As the hospital was used as a neuropsychiatric unit for the hospitals of the 12th Hospital Center an assortment of cases were received who did not need to be in a specialised N.P. Hospital. This local use by the Hospital Center tended to interfere with the larger mission of the 96th which was to serve the entire European Theatre. The 96th was the only general hospital in the E.T.O. dealing exclusively with N.P. patients until the 130th General Hospital, N.P. was established in Belgium towards the end of the war.

Alongside the treatment of patients at the hospital, several of the psychiatrists conducted research into some of the symptoms displayed by the patients. To counteract the prevalent feeling that neuropsychiatric casualties were merely ineffective soldiers Captain William P. Kapuler conducted a study of a group of neuropsychiatric patients who had been cited for bravery in combat. A group of personnel studied combat reactions in patients such as amnesia, regression, hallucination in the hopes of finding more effective treatment. Captain Harold Rosen carried out studies on patients suffering from 'mixed personalities' and paranoia. Captain Jack Hartman studied a number of prisoners who could not

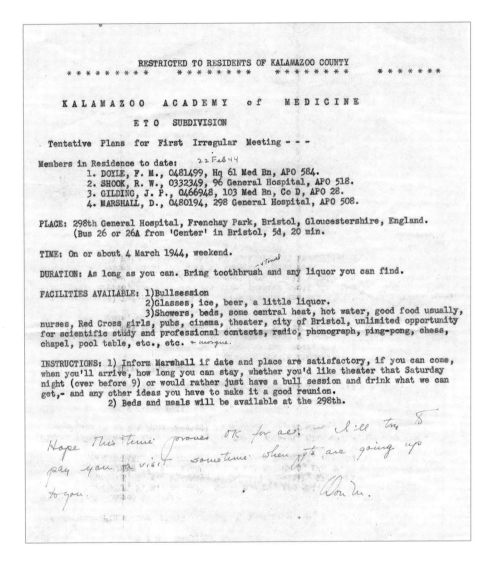

RESTRICTED TO RESIDENTS OF KALAMAZOO COUNTY

* * * * * * * *   * * * * * * *   * * * * * * *   * * * * * *

K A L A M A Z O O   A C A D E M Y   o f   M E D I C I N E

E T O   SUBDIVISION

Tentative Plans for First Irregular Meeting - - -

Members in Residence to date: 22 Feb 44
    1. DOYLE, F. M., 0481499, Hq 61 Med Bn, APO 584.
    2. SHOOK, R. W., 0332349, 96 General Hospital, APO 518.
    3. GILDING, J. P., 0466948, 103 Med Bn, Co D, APO 28.
    4. MARSHALL, D., 0480194, 298 General Hospital, APO 508.

PLACE: 298th General Hospital, Frenchay Park, Bristol, Gloucestershire, England.
    (Bus 26 or 26A from 'Center' in Bristol, 5d, 20 min.

TIME: On or about 4 March 1944, weekend.

DURATION: As long as you can. Bring toothbrush and any liquor you can find.

FACILITIES AVAILABLE: 1) Bullsession
                  2) Glasses, ice, beer, a little liquor.
                  3) Showers, beds, some central heat, hot water, good food usually,
nurses, Red Cross girls, pubs, cinema, theater, city of Bristol, unlimited opportunity
for scientific study and professional contacts, radio, phonograph, ping-pong, chess,
chapel, pool table, etc., etc. + morgue.

INSTRUCTIONS: 1) Inform Marshall if date and place are satisfactory, if you can come,
when you'll arrive, how long you can stay, whether you'd like theater that Saturday
night (over before 9) or would rather just have a bull session and drink what we can
get,- and any other ideas you have to make it a good reunion.
              2) Beds and meals will be available at the 298th.

*Hope this time proves OK for all - I'll try to
pay you a visit sometime when you are going up
to you.*
                                        Don M.

*Letter received by Dr Ralph Shook notifying him of meeting
at Frenchay Hospital (J. Shock).*

remember their crimes which ranged from being AWOL to rape and manslaughter. The truth drug, sodium amytal was administered in various doses to the prisoners. In six cases full confession of the "forgotten incidents" was obtained. Some of the personnel also led investigations into identical twins and differences in their psychiatric make up. The 96th was also designated as an observation and recommendation centre for homosexuals.

The personnel did have some off duty time, particularly in the period before D-Day. Unlike the patients the medical personnel were allowed off base and Dr. Ralph Shook took advantage of this to meet up with some of his colleagues from his home town of Kalamazoo, Michigan. The four doctors met up in March 1944 at Frenchay Hospital in Bristol where Dr. Marshall was based. The group produced minutes of their meeting, written tongue in cheek, comparing life back in the U.S. to their life in a military hospital in the U.K. They included such comments as:

"Whereas we have the opportunity of enjoying the invigorating climate and cool fresh air of England, our less fortunate associates at home are forced to work in overheated offices and to relax in hot night clubs."

Their minutes finish with the statement:

"The next meeting will depend on Ike and his boys."

It appears the imminent invasion of the continent was to prevent any more meetings.

Chapter 3

CRUSHED BY THE
JUGGERNAUTS OF WAR

In the months leading up to the D-Day invasion the hospital made arrangements to receive larger numbers of patients. In April 1944 the hospital was informed of the 'Tented Expansion Program.' This involved fitting specially made tented structures to the end of the wards to create more bed space. Sufficient tents were erected although the personnel felt that it would be inadvisable to treat N.P. patients in tents if it could be avoided. Therefore, after consulting the Surgeon, Western Base Section, it was decided to make 173 double decked bunk beds so that extra patients could be placed in the existing wards.

Motor Pool at 96th General Hospital (96th General Hospital Year Book).

¾ ton Dodge WC51 being serviced by mechanics (96th General Hospital Year Book).

Plans were made for the admittance of several hundred patients at one time by the Receiving Officer, Captain Clifford Keidel, but these were found to be unnecessary as the greatest number of patients admitted in one day was 127 on 8 August 1944.

As expected, after D-Day there was an increase in the patient load. The hospital found that it was necessary to adapt their procedures to cope with the numbers and also to handle the different types of neuropsychiatric patients that were now arriving at the hospital.

On D-Day plus 10 the first trainload of patients from Normandy arrived at the hospital. They were examined and found to have different symptoms to the pre-invasion patients. For the majority of the medical staff it was their first experience of caring for combat cases. There had been no indication from the higher authorities as to what part the 96th was to play in treating combat cases so it was decided that the hospital should make combat patients the priority while putting its function as a holding hospital for men who were to return home secondary.

The hospital was soon filled to capacity, even with the use of double decked bunks so it became necessary to establish a waiting list for patients waiting to be admitted from the N.P. wards of other general hospitals. As the number of psychiatric patients in the European Theatre of Operations increased there became a greater need for more psychiatrists in regular general hospitals. The 96th served as a training centre for personnel from general hospitals with neuropsychiatric sections. During this period it was often necessary for general hospitals to hold and carry out evacuation board proceedings for psychotic patients.

A few days after the first trainload of patients arrived at Brickbarns there was a large influx of combat cases. It was thought best to keep the combat cases separate from those awaiting transport to the Zone of the Interior as about twenty percent of the combat cases were treatable and would be returned to duty. It was also necessary to organise a combat section within the Psychiatric Service which would have its own admission, Treatment and Disposition wards. As Colonel Smith commented in the archives:

"This section strained the physical resources of the hospital as well as the ingenuity of the medical staff in providing for their care" (96th General Hospital Archives).

Because of the large number of patients in the hospital the three medical officers assigned to the Treatment Section could not manage to see all of the patients often enough so it was decided that patients receiving modified Insulin or Electric Shock on their wards should remain in the care of their respected ward officers. The ward officers would also treat patients needing individual psychotherapy. This left the medical officers free to act in an advisory capacity.

Board Meeting taking place in one of the wards. Lt. Col. Keine, Capt, Kennedy and Capt. Ellis determine if a patient should be sent back to duty or back to the United States for additional treatment (96th General Hospital Year Book).

Because of the number of combat cases showing signs of being able to return to duty it was decided to enlarge the rehabilitation programme. The programme was extended to include everyone capable of participating in it. Even closed ward cases had a rehabilitation programme that included daily calisthenics, close order drills, arts, crafts, games and watching movies.

The Open Ward patients were expected to carry out tasks throughout the hospital. There were 198 jobs in the hospital which could be filled by patients as part of their rehabilitation. These included Kitchen Police, Mess hall guards, clerks, gardeners and ward maintenance men. Before patients were allocated these jobs they were assessed by a group consisting of Psychiatrist, Psychologist, and Rehabilitation Department Officer. Patients carrying out assignments were rewarded with privileges.

Rehabilitation for combat cases was held in two wards isolated from the rest of the hospital. Originally they had been Disposition Wards but now they became known as the Recovery Wing and were treated like barracks from 28 June 1944 onwards. The archivist describes the format of the Recovery Wing:

"Here were housed patients destined to return to some form of duty in a short time. Upon arrival at the Recovery Wing the candidates were clothed in fatigue uniforms, which was part of the plan to remove the patients from the hospital atmosphere. Sick call was held each morning and this was the only contact the candidates had with a medical officer during their stay in the Recovery wing. Fashioned after the Army basic training plan, a program of military training which included drill and calisthenics, marches off the post and classes of military subjects was put into operation. A large portion of the time was allotted to outdoor activities which has as its primary purpose the physical reconditioning of the soldier so that he could return to full duty or to a non-combat job in the European Theatre of Operation in the best physical condition" (96th General Hospital Archives).

In the early part of August 1944 the Rehabilitation Department utilised three infantry officers from the Officer patient personnel who had seen front line combat in Normandy to command the men in the Recovery Wing. Under their direction a gymnasium was erected with material salvaged from scrap lumber. With the cooperation of the Special Service Department parallel bars, gym mats, punch bags, ping pong tables and other sports equipment were secured. The Red Cross worked with the Rehabilitation Section to order sports equipment and also to set up a nurses' softball team. Upon completion the gymnasium was also able to serve as a classroom and dayroom for patients.

In July 1944 60 percent of patients in the Recovery Wing were returned to duty and this rose to 92 percent in September. After September the type of patients arriving at the hospital changed markedly and many were not suited to a Recovery Wing Programme. This was partly because other general hospitals receiving neuropsychiatric combat cases were able to put them through their own rehabilitation programmes and return them to duty, only those with neuropsychiatric symptoms who could not be sent back into the armed services were sent to the 96th.

Lieutenant S. of the 1st Infantry Division was such a case. He was admitted to the 96th General Hospital in April 1945. He had gone ashore with the first wave on Omaha Beach on D-Day. Most of his men had been casualties and he believed that he should have been killed. He stated:

"Germans sitting there waiting for us, no man has a right to come out alive."

He had adjusted to the combat experience, he stated that he had normal fear but he had been able to control it.

Patients from the Recovery wing in fatigue uniforms (96th General Hospital Year Book).

After this experience he developed a feeling of personal vulnerability which was reinforced when he saw so many others become casualties. His onset of symptoms of anxiety was gradual. He had battle dreams, was nervous, irritable and had difficulty sleeping while in England awaiting the invasion but he first noticed symptoms of extreme anxiety in August 1944 at Mayenne. His outfit had been spread over a large area when reports came in that an attack by S.S. troops was imminent. This was followed by another report that S.S. Paratroopers had landed behind his outfit. The attack did not materialise but much tension had been built up and the Lieutenant started to be apprehensive about making decisions which may be costly to his men.

In September 1944 he was hit by shrapnel and was knocked down twice by the concussion. He managed to crawl to an aid station from where he was evacuated to Britain. He returned to duty in January 1945 but his anxiety symptoms and depression got increasingly worse. On 24 February he was admitted to a 1st Division Rear Aid Station for an upper respiratory tract infection. On 26 February he was sent to 76th General Hospital in Paris where a diagnosis of psychoneurosis and reactive depression was made. He was evacuated to the United Kingdom and admitted to the 34th General Hospital, a holding unit on 20 March. On 21 March he was transferred to the

Letter sent from the 96th General Hospital at Brickbarns (Authors' collection).

93rd General Hospital in Malvern where a Disposition Board met and made the same diagnosis as had been made at the 62nd. On 5 April he was admitted to the 96th General Hospital where his treatment continued while he awaited transport back to the U.S.

His principal symptoms at this time were nervousness, anxiety, fatigability, irritability, depression, insomnia and battle dreams. He was indecisive, uncertain and insecure. He felt that his illness was due to 120 days continuous combat as a Rifle Platoon Leader and worry over the heavy casualties in his unit. He stated that he had lost confidence in himself and he felt that he could not train troops anymore because of his hatred for guns. He was shipped back to the U.S. and on 5 May he arrived at the Station Hospital at Camp Kilmer, New Jersey, from here he was sent to Wakeman Convalescent Hospital.

Chapter 4

LAST VOYAGE OF THE U.S.S. RICH

U.S.S. Rich underway somewhere in the Atlantic (E. Black).

Ed Black arrived as a patient at the 96th General Hospital on July 4 1944 in an unconscious state. He had been aboard the U.S.S. Rich, D.E. 695, when it was sunk by mines off the coast of Normandy on 8 June 1944.

Until the beginning of June 1944 the U.S.S. Rich had the role of scout ship in convoys sailing across the Atlantic Ocean from New York to Londonderry in Northern Ireland and back again. The zigzag route across the Atlantic took about fourteen days and upon arrival at Londonderry the men were given a few days Liberty before returning to the States.

On arrival at Londonderry docks the radio room was secured. No messages could be retrieved while it was docked so Ed's daily task was to pick up messages for the Rich from the navy radio station on shore. The messages were decoded back aboard ship.

On the afternoon of June 2 Ed collected the messages as usual, noticing that this time they were marked 'Urgent'. On reaching the ship Ed handed the messages to Lieutenant Enquist for decoding. When the Lieutenant returned from decoding the message his expression was grave. All Liberty was cancelled and M.P.s were sent to recall all men who had gone ashore. Within 45 minutes the crew were all aboard and the skipper, Lieutenant Commander Edward A. Michel Jr. informed the men that the Rich had been chosen to participate in the Normandy Invasion. Another Destroyer escort, the U.S.S. Bunch, DE694, had been assigned to the mission but had encountered mechanical problems in port. U.S.S. Rich had been chosen to take her place.

After being loaded with ammunition, the Rich sailed down through the Irish Sea to Plymouth where extra guns were loaded. While the guns were being installed the crew were told to move to the starboard side of the ship to avoid conversation with the men who came aboard. Once the Rich had docked at Plymouth the men were confined to the ship.

The Rich was assigned to act as escort for the battleship U.S.S. Nevada, a veteran of Pearl Harbor. The ships departed from Plymouth with expectations of invading on June 5 but because of the poor weather on that day it was necessary for the Rich to wait a day in the English Channel along with the rest of the convoy of over 4,000 ships. Barrage balloons were tied above the ships to deter German aircraft.

The ships approached the beaches at approximately 2a.m. French time on June 6. Ed remembers the scene vividly:

Ed Black on his 20th birthday. (E. Black).

"The skies were ablaze with anti-aircraft fire. It looked like hell on earth. Gasoline dumps were going up, hit by Allied bombs. I wondered if any living thing could be left and if there was any point in invading."

As the crew of the Rich took bombardment positions (Ed and 11 others on the 1.1 gun) they watched 37 C47 transports flying over, each towing gliders. Five were hit by German anti-aircraft batteries. Ed remembers that they seemed to disintegrate in the air. He recalls:

"At 6.40a.m. all hell broke loose. The U.S.S. Quincy fired the first salvo on the beaches, then the other ships began laying salvos in; U.S.S. Bayfield was loaded with

Left: Two U.S.S. Rich crew members on liberty in Londonderry, Ireland. On the left is Walter Hibyan, MM 1/c. On the right is Edmund Kozlik, MM 1/c. Kozlik was killed in action on June 8th, 1944. (E. Black) Right: Radio room aboard the U.S.S. Rich. At the radio controls is RM3/c Richard Fisher. Seated in the radio room, doorway is S2/c Edwin B. Black (E. Black).

Several U.S.S. Rich crew members on liberty in Londonderry, Ireland. The crewman on the extreme left is Wt 3/c John F. Warne. Third from the left is F 1/c Richard Vanderwende. Both Warne and Vanderwende were killed in action on June 8th, 1944. (E. Black).

troops, nets were lowered to the water and the weary soldiers began climbing down to enter Higgins boats for the trip to the beaches. Each Higgins boat carried 27 men in full battle gear. The trip was just under 4 miles, a rough ride through swampy water. Suddenly German aircraft appeared overhead in an attempt to drop a bomb on the Nevada. It fell short and dropped to our port side, barely missing us by 100 yards. It fell into the centre of a Higgins boat which had just left the Bayfield. Twenty seven men died before they saw the sandy soil of Omaha Beach. Guns, helmets, pieces of the Higgins boat and men blew upward into the air. Very soon the waters were filled with the dead. The heat of the battle made any attempts to recover casualties impossible."

At dusk the Rich laid a smoke screen along the beaches to foil attacking German S. boats. Around 9p.m. the crew saw a torpedo wave coming within a few feet of the ship on the port side. In seconds there was a muffled roar and hiss of steam from the U.S.S. Meredith, which had been lying behind the Rich, as she sank below the surface.

The battle continued through the day and night of June 7. On the morning of June 8 Ed wrote in his diary:

"We are all thanking God that we went through the night without a mishap. During the time since the invasion started we have slept only a few hours and eaten very little food. All of us are nervous and jumpy. At the present time the U.S.S. Nevada, the ship we are protecting, is shelling a town over on the coast with her large guns. If we come through this O.K. we will be lucky. However our trust is in God to take us through safely."

At around 8.45 a.m. on June 8 the Rich was ordered to proceed to Utah beach to render aid to the Destroyer U.S.S. Glennon, DD620, which had struck a mine North West of the Saint Marcouf Islands, near Utah Beach. As the Rich approached the Glennon the ship was seen to be half submerged in the water with a towboat hook on its bow. A few of the personnel were on deck. The Rich dispatched a whale boat but the Glennon signalled that no help was needed and to look out for mines. The Rich then moved to take up station ahead of the minesweeper, Staff, which had taken the Glennon in tow.

When the Rich was about 300 yards from the minesweeper, at approximately 9.20a.m. a mine exploded 50 yards off Rich's starboard beam. This tripped circuit breakers, knocked out the ship's lighting and knocked sailors off their feet but caused no structural damage. Three minutes later a second mine went off directly under the ship. Approximately 50 feet of her stern was blown off and floated away on fire, sinking slowly.

As the men picked themselves up and examined themselves for injuries there was a third explosion under the ship. The blast blew Ed straight up in the air. This explosion destroyed the forward section of the ship, the flying bridge was demolished, the forward fire room severely damaged and the mast toppled.

Of the 12 men posted on the 1.1 gun nine lay dead. Ed and a colleague, Carlie Black were both badly wounded but decided they should try to jump from the sinking ship. The word to abandon ship was being passed around

Photographs showing the U.S.S. Rich striking the mine that broke her back.
(N. Fuller).

by word of mouth because the loud speaker system had been knocked out. The two men locked arms and jumped from the boat deck on the starboard side. They managed to reach a six man life raft and hook their arms into the lines. This is the last Ed remembers as he spent the next 31 days unconscious. Four of the men he shared the life raft with died within the next few hours aboard LST567 which picked them up from the water. This included Ed's colleague, Carlie Black.

A few minutes after Ed had abandoned ship the Rich went down. Out of a crew of 215, 89 officers and men were lost with the ship, 56 survivors were wounded and 62 were missing. The U.S.S. Rich was the only American Destroyer Escort lost from the invasion force. LCDR Michel was awarded the Navy Cross for 'extraordinary heroism and devotion to duty'. The citation concludes:

"Lieutenant Commander Michel, despite severe injuries, including a broken leg, steadfastly refused to leave his ship, and directed and assisted in the removal of all possible survivors until his ship sank beneath him. By his action and example all able bodied survivors on board were inspired to remain with the ship and assist in the rescue of the greatest possible number of men."

When he reached land Ed was taken to a British hospital and then, while still unconscious, transferred to the 96th General Hospital. He was sent to a neuropsychiatric hospital because of his serious head injuries. The medical personnel had little hope that his brain would function normally when he regained consciousness.

A few days after his arrival at the 96th Ed regained consciousness. At first he thought he had been captured and was in a P.O.W. hospital. On the second day he was given shock treatment. When he came round the doctor asked him a few simple questions like 'How many wheels does a bicycle have?' and 'How many wheels does a wagon have?' when Ed answered correctly the doctor

Left: Approximately 0920 hours, 8.06.44, near Utah Beach. The U.S.S. Rich is moving into position to assist the U.S.S. Glennon. Minutes after this picture was taken, the Rich struck her first mine. (E. Black) Centre: U.S.S. Rich striking the mine that broke her back. (N. Fuller) Right: Crew member, Dan Westcott receiving a light after rescue. (E.Black).

O.S. Rescu Flotilla One   K. P. Schoop-rd, Ens (R), U.S.C.G.,

Eye witness account of the sinking of the U.S.S. Rich
as recorded in the ship's log of the minesweeper.

suggested that he could be transferred to the 155th General Hospital at Blackmore Park as he would not need neuropsychiatric treatment. However Ed asked if he could remain at the 96th to avoid the upheaval of moving hospitals. Ed was surprised to find himself in an army hospital rather than a navy hospital. On arrival at the hospital he had nothing, all his possessions had gone down with the ship and his uniform was in tatters. The hospital provided him with an army uniform but he had no money and navy personnel could not draw pay from an army hospital at that time Fortunately the captain in the bed next to him gave him money for stamps and anything else he needed. Ed was unsure of how to address the senior officers at the hospital and was reprimanded for calling Colonel Smith 'Mister' instead of 'Sir'.

Ed had multiple injuries. His leg was broken and he was in a body cast. He had brain concussion, a skull fracture, a damaged right eye, his teeth and part of his gum and lip were missing and his jaw was broken in five places. He remembers passing out while his jaw was being wired up. Because of his injuries Ed had little mobility. A medic pushed him round the hospital site in a wheelchair and when Ed commented on the beauty of the Malvern Hills he offered to push him up to the top, but the offer was not taken up.

Ed remained in the hospital until August 18 1944 when he was sent back to the U.S. He travelled by ambulance to Birmingham and then by train to Liverpool where he boarded the U.S.S. West Point (formerly the S.S. America). Three days into the journey to Boston there was a smell of burning rubber and Ed was told that the engine room had caught fire. It burned for three hours before it was put out. Fortunately there was no serious damage and the incident only delayed the voyage by one day.

Once he arrived in the U.S. Ed was taken by ambulance to the Chelsea Navy Hospital just outside Boston. He was the first Normandy invasion Navy casualty to arrive there. At first the doctors thought that he was an infantry soldier as he was still wearing the army uniform he had been given at the 96th.

Forty years later, on the anniversary of D-Day, Ed was standing on Utah Beach, looking out to the spot where the Rich sank when a man called his name. Ed's name was printed on the back of his jacket and the man recognised it as he was the one who had pulled him off the life raft and into the L.S.T. As Frank Calvo had cut Ed's clothes off him to treat his injuries Ed's diary had fallen out of his pocket. Frank had picked it up and kept it because he thought that Ed would die from the severe injuries he had sustained. Back in America Frank was able to return the diary to Ed.

In 2004 Ed Black was awarded the French Legion of Honour for his part in the Normandy landings.

Chapter 5

RESTRICTED RECREATION

During the latter part of January 1944 a Red Cross Group was assigned to the 96th General Hospital. Like the personnel at the parent unit the girls were expecting to be working at a regular general hospital and already had a programme planned with this in mind. Milda Cohen, the Assistant Field Director records that;

" … it came as a shock and disappointment for the workers who had been thinking and planning in terms of a program for a general hospital" (96th A.R.C. Archives).

With the exception of Milda Cohen, none of the girls had had any real contact or experience with neuropsychiatric patients and even Milda Cohen's experience was very limited. The Head Recreation Worker, Mary Moss, wrote in her report:

"To work out a program for mental patients is a challenge to trained personnel and to those of us who have not had training or experience in psychiatric work the job is overwhelming" (96th A.R.C. Archives).

However the work of the Red Cross unit was to be vital at Brickbarns. All the patients were restricted to the post and had no other form of recreation. Because of the nature of the hospital the Red Cross work was subject to limitations and one of these was that the girls were not permitted to work on the wards.

For Open Ward patients this was not a problem as most were ambulatory and had access to the Red Cross building which was a converted ward. Milda Cohen describes it in the Red Cross archives:

"The building consists of a very large bright airy recreation room and a series of smaller rooms. There is an office for the secretary, AFD and recreation workers, a craft shop, a library, a storeroom and another room which is to be used for a music room and also a room where patients may entertain their visitors, as there is no other place in the camp for this purpose" (96th A.R.C. Archives).

The group had difficulty in furnishing the rooms as when they approached the Special Service Officer who was distributing the furniture assigned to the hospital he said that he felt that:

" … the patients would abuse the furniture and it would not hold up under their use" (96th A.R.C. Archives).

At this the Red Cross decided to consult the Executive Officer, Lieutenant Colonel McCloud, who arranged for the girls to have a number of benches and six comfortable chairs to replace the '*unsightly, soiled beach chairs*' the unit had been using. The girls also ordered rugs, card tables and a radiogram to furnish the building.

The Red Cross received a number of new phonographs to use at the hospital but they had:

" *... very inadequate springs and are hardly worth the trouble and expense to have them shipped over*" *(96th A.R.C. Archives)*.

Because they were American made the girls could not replace the springs. They also complained that they were:

" *... tinny in sound and unless it is a hot jive number without much melody they do not sound too good even when they are new*" *(96th A.R.C. Archives)*.

The Red Cross had the use of a patient detail to clean their building as part of the rehabilitation programme but because of the rapid turn over of patients at the hospital there was a constant change of personnel in the details and some weeks there was no cleaning detail at all. When there was a cleaning detail it was necessary for the men to be supervised by a member of the Red Cross at all times as:

" *... for the most part they are easily distracted and lose interest in the job on hand*" *(96th A.R.C. Archives)*.

Milda Cohen admitted that:

" *... it is true that the building often looks as though a cyclone had struck it. We try to encourage the patients to be careful with cigarette ashes, papers, magazines etc. but ... *" *(96th A.R.C. Archives)*.

For the Closed Wards it was decided that the Red Cross could furnish the materials for the patients to use under the nurses' supervision. This was not an entirely satisfactory situation so individual ward officers negotiated for the Red Cross workers to handle a number of 'approved activities' on the ward. The girls arranged for books and games to be distributed and provided the materials for bingo parties to be run by the nurse on the ward.

Each afternoon a group of 65-85 Closed Ward patients were permitted to spend two hours in the Recreation Hall accompanied by corpsmen. During this time the men were allowed to work on individual

Lt. Col. Ben L. McCloud Executive Officer (96th General Hospital Year Book).

Patients sitting on beach chairs in Library (96th General Hospital Year Book).

craft work, although this was limited by the patient's attention span. As Mary Moss comments:

"Our patients, of course, cannot be held accountable for their actions and ideas so we find that many projects are left unfinished and much material wasted. We must be on constant watch as this type of patient has no regard for property or property rights" (96th A.R.C. Archives).

In March 1944 a new regulation was introduced, that patients must be back on their wards from 7.00p.m. onwards. As patients were not allowed to use the Red Cross rooms until 1.00p.m., this only gave a short time to accommodate both open and closed ward patients who were not permitted to mix. In April a ruling was introduced that prohibited the use of the Red Cross building from 4.00p.m. to 5.00p.m. as some patients were arriving late at the Mess Hall.

In April Milda Cohen notes that:

"We find a great deal of resentment on the part of the patients who are not allowed to use the R.C. building as they normally have in other set ups" (hospitals) *(96th A.R.C. Archives).*

Unfortunately, in May an E.T.O. ruling put another restriction on Red Cross activities when it prohibited the use of wards as Red Cross buildings. This was probably because it was thought that all wards would be needed for casualties from the imminent invasion. In exchange the girls were offered a third of the space in the Patient's Recreation Building and a tar paper building which had been used to store groceries.

In the latter part of June the Red Cross moved to the Patient's Recreation building which was not a very satisfactory arrangement as the large recreation room was also used for movies three nights a week. This necessitated a complete rearrangement of the room every night. Richard Lloyd remembers that some of the local children would be allowed to come and watch the movies with the personnel of the 96th.

The rear of the building was partitioned to make two offices, one for the secretary and the other for the A.F.D. A portion off the Utilities building was set up as a studio and craft shop. Closed Ward patients were not allowed to work in the studio because of the tools used there.

Because of the nature of the hospital Milda Cohen had a constant flow of patients arriving at her office with problems and it was left to her to explain why so many restrictions had been imposed on them, such as not being allowed passes, not having access to their personal possessions and not being paid.

The patients were only allowed visits from relatives while at the hospital. Fiancées were not included in this category. Servicemen were not permitted to marry while they were patients at the hospital and this caused a number of problems as some patients who had made plans to marry before they were hospitalised were now required to postpone their wedding until after their return to the U.S. In one case the wedding date had been fixed for the week after the patient's admission. In these situations it was the task of the Red Cross to help the servicemen face this fact and encourage him to write or phone his fiancée. In some cases the Red Cross workers took it upon themselves to explain the situation to the fiancées. Immigration rules were explained should the girl wish to follow the patient to the States. This situation was further complicated if the fiancées were pregnant. The Social Worker reported that several illegitimate children were born in these circumstances.

Milda Cohen believed that the reason for the large number of patients arriving at her door with problems was because:

" ... there has been a general tendency to refer problems to the Red Cross where there is a conflict over an established policy or when no particular policy has been established" (96th A.R.C. Archives).

Unbeknown to the girls at the 96th, complaints from the patients about the Red Cross unit dealing with these issues were being investigated in the U.S. from April 1944 onwards. The five main complaints from the patients were:

1. *That the Red Cross personnel in that hospital just do not bother, 'go on Red Cross reputation', have little interest in taking time to let a man talk over what worries him, frequently permit interviews to be interrupted by telephone calls of a definitely personal nature etc.*

2. *That the recreation program is inadequate and little effort is made to provide simple but interesting activities for the men.*

3. *That there is discrimination in the giving out of gum and other small supplies, e.g. one man 'who stands in well' will be given some after a group has been told that there is no more despite the fact that the latter can clearly see the supplies on the shelves.*

4. *That the personnel appear more interested in 'dating' than in the job and pay attention chiefly to the officers.*

5. *That the staff watches the clock and frequently closes up a few minutes ahead of time (96th A.R.C. Archives).*

The complaints went first to the office of the Field Director in Massachusetts and were then sent to the Area Supervisor of the American Red Cross Headquarters in Washington D.C. and then to the Commissioner of the American Red Cross based in London. The Commissioner and Field supervisor wrote replies to the American Red Cross Headquarters in Washington, informing the Vice Chairman that the 96th was a neuropsychiatric hospital and it was possible that complaints were down to:

" ... *the nature of the difficulties of those men who have not been able to make an army adjustment and their added anxieties and sense of urgency about returning to the States*"

The Field Supervisor added that:

" ... *many are extremely attention demanding and rather unreasonable about what Red Cross workers should be doing for them about their situation*" *(96th A.R.C. Archives).*

The Commissioner, Harvey Gibson, concludes his letter with the comment:

"*We do not believe that you need to be overly concerned with complaints from those returning who have been interned there*" *(96th A.R.C. Archives).*

This reply was then sent back through the channels with the comments added that the Field Director, Mary Louise Burns, who first passed on the complaints should have made it clear that the complaints came from neuropsychiatric patients. It appears that the matter was laid to rest at this point but in July 1944, on the recommendation of Colonel Smith and the Red Cross Field Supervisor, a new Red Cross unit was installed at the 96th. Four members of the original unit left for reassignment with Red Cross elsewhere, only Mary Priebe, the Staff Aide was retained.

On 15 July Dora McMullen was assigned Assistant Field Director at the 96th. She was joined by five new assignments, bringing the Red Cross unit numbers up to seven.

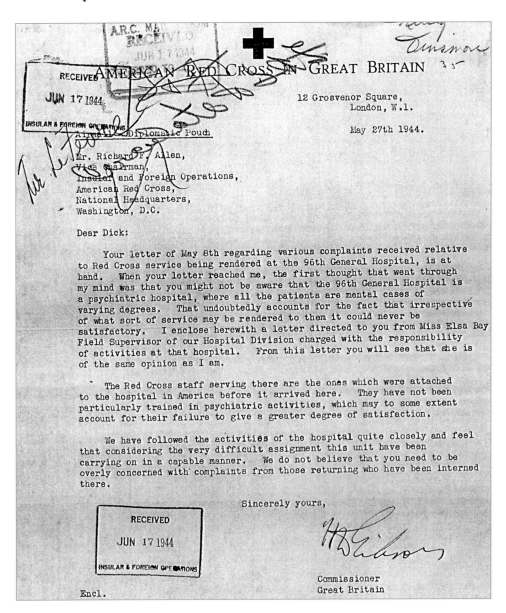

AMERICAN RED CROSS IN GREAT BRITAIN

RECEIVED
JUN 17 1944
INSULAR & FOREIGN OPERATIONS

12 Grosvenor Square,
London, W.1.

May 27th 1944.

Mr. Richard F. Allen,
Vice Chairman,
Insular and Foreign Operations,
American Red Cross,
National Headquarters,
Washington, D.C.

Dear Dick:

Your letter of May 8th regarding various complaints received relative to Red Cross service being rendered at the 96th General Hospital, is at hand. When your letter reached me, the first thought that went through my mind was that you might not be aware that the 96th General Hospital is a psychiatric hospital, where all the patients are mental cases of varying degrees. That undoubtedly accounts for the fact that irrespective of what sort of service may be rendered to them it could never be satisfactory. I enclose herewith a letter directed to you from Miss Elsa Bay Field Supervisor of our Hospital Division charged with the responsibility of activities at that hospital. From this letter you will see that she is of the same opinion as I am.

The Red Cross staff serving there are the ones which were attached to the hospital in America before it arrived here. They have not been particularly trained in psychiatric activities, which may to some extent account for their failure to give a greater degree of satisfaction.

We have followed the activities of the hospital quite closely and feel that considering the very difficult assignment this unit have been carrying on in a capable manner. We do not believe that you need to be overly concerned with complaints from those returning who have been interned there.

Sincerely yours,

RECEIVED
JUN 17 1944
INSULAR & FOREIGN OPERATIONS

Encl.

Commissioner
Great Britain

Letter from the Red Cross Commissioner to American Red Cross Headquarters in Washington D.C. (96th A.R.C. Archives).

Chapter 6

'THE A.R.C. IS ON PARADE'

The new members of the Red Cross unit found that they were working with the same restrictions of time and space that the former members had. Dora McMullen found that the patients reacted to the new group of Red Cross in much the same way as they had to the previous unit. In her monthly report she comments on the comparison between working in this hospital and in a regular general hospital:

"There is more hostility expressed towards the workers and the lack of passes, few, if any, visitors and multiple restrictions of the post irk the patients and are reflected in the actions of the patients in our programs. A large proportion of the patients are those who have not adjusted to army life and their lack of adaptation is expressed in a negative attitude towards any program which is attempted. This negative and sometimes hostile attitude towards the program requires staff members who can understand the hostility and bear up under it" (96th A.R.C. Archives).

Red Cross unit: Evelyn Edelson, Marion Hogan, Bertha Ellingson,
Mary Priebe, Mary Gormley, Nan Burgess (96th General Hospital Year Book).

Another problem Dora McMullen came across was:

" *... the amount of time that is consumed by patients whose problems etc. are fantasy and the amount of checking that is necessary before the actual work can be done. For example concern about home problems may have originated from delusions of persecution thus the time spent with each individual man has to be longer and in many instances draws a blank"* (96th A.R.C. Archives).

A more productive service the Red Cross was able to offer was 'letter writing'. Letters were written for illiterate patients such as two black soldiers who were being treated at the 96th, but literate patients were encouraged to write their own, with Red Cross support, as letter writing was thought to be of therapeutic value. Dora McMullen records:

"In five cases patients whose nervous conditions made letter writing impossible for them were assisted and encouraged until they demonstrated that they could take care of their correspondence themselves. One of these at first claimed that he could not only write because he was too confused to organise his thinking, but he was too nervous even to copy the letter after the worker composed it for him. The worker asked him to make an attempt promising that if he failed she would recopy it. After two hours of effort the patient copied the brief note and an appointment was made for another letter to be written a week later. The patient waited four days and then came back for his second letter which he not only copied but enlarged upon. The fifth letter was written by the patient alone under the worker's supervision. ... Four patients who received assistance with letter writing showed no improvement and had to be helped with each letter until the patient was evacuated" (96th A.R.C. Archives).

Sometimes requests to help with letter writing could lead to discussion of other issues that were making the patient anxious. Bertha Ellingson (Staff

*Letter sent from the American Red Cross at the
96th General Hospital (Authors' collection).*

Social Worker) recounts her progress with 'Sgt. G.' who was a patient on a closed ward. He had asked a nurse to request that a Red Cross worker help him write a letter.

"He seemed quite rational, said he had not written for 'I don't know how long but it must be a couple of months' and now he wanted to let his wife know that he was getting along alright. The message having been composed, the patient told his story.

He did not recall leaving the front. When he first gained consciousness he believed himself to be among Germans. He refused to let the doctor and nurses treat him. He struck an American nurse. Now he was ashamed. Assured that the nurse understood he went on to tell that he had been give treatment forcibly. 'I've been through hell and back on this cot. Every time they took me for treatment I thought I was going to my execution. I was sure they were all Germans.' He told me of hallucinations, auditory and visual. To the worker's attempt at reassurance he replied: 'but you don't understand. I used to work in a mental hospital. What will my future be? Will I be able to work again? Will there be recurrences?" (96th A.R.C. Archives).

Bertha Ellingson attempted to reassure him and encouraged him to talk his fears over with the psychiatrist. A week later he met the social worker and told her he had had no further hallucinations. He was considerably less anxious about his recovery. He wanted to discuss another issue that was on his conscience. He explained that he had been a medic with a unit on the continent when he had killed three Germans. When the social worker heard the circumstances she reassured him that his actions had been justified and that as no charge had been brought against him by this time there would be no punishment. She encouraged him to talk to his doctor about the matter.

In October 1944 the Red Cross were able to offer another facility to the patients of the 96th in the shape of a Public Address System. At the beginning of November the Colonel and Special Service Officer met with the Red Cross unit to decide how the programme for the P.A. should be organised. It was decided that the weekly programme should include; patient talent, special shows, Red Cross announcements, a Request programme and Chaplain's Devotions. In December the P.A. was well used as Christmas festivities were announced.

Three weeks before Christmas materials were distributed to each ward for the patients to make decorations. Special Service gave each ward a tree. The contest ended on the evening of December 23 when the judges toured the wards. The prizes, which were ward parties, were awarded to the best open and closed wards.

Various buildings around the site were decorated. The Red Cross building had a false ceiling of red and green crepe paper, window friezes of bells and

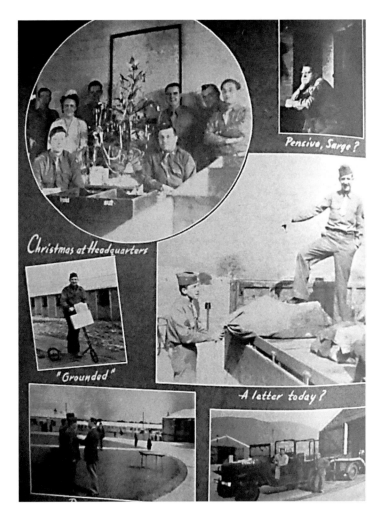

Christmas preparations at the 96th. (96th General Hospital Year Book).

trees, large red bells suspended from the ceiling and silver and gold stars hanging all over the room. A large Christmas tree stood in one corner decorated with glittered ping pong balls and tin foil icicles as well as a few regular ornaments. On the wall was a map of the United States outlined in holly with postcards from home filling the map.

On December 18 there was a dance for the enlisted men of the command at the Officer's Club. The dance band from the 55th General Hospital was hired and a buffet supper was served from 10-11p.m. British service girls were invited to the dance.

Christmas boxes were given out on Christmas Eve by Santa Claus and the Red Cross Staff. The Red Cross buildings were closed so that all the wards could be visited between 7p.m. and 11p.m. Santa managed to shake hands with practically every man in the hospital and Christmas boxes were even given to the new admissions to the hospital who arrived at 12.30a.m. Christmas morning.

On Christmas Day the Red Cross Staff worked at the Patient's Mess which they had decorated, one room in white and green and one in white and blue. The girls served coffee and passed out fruit, wishing Merry Christmas to all the patients.

On New Year's Eve the girls threw a party for the patients:

" ... the only drawback being the hours from 6 to 8p.m. However we managed to instil a jovial spirit into the guests so that Auld Lang Syne was struck at 7.45p.m. and every one was wishing everyone else a Happy New Year on coffee" (96th A.R.C. Archives).

In the new year a popular activity in the evenings in the Red Cross Rooms was Bingo Parties:

"In order to interest more parties and let each feel that he has won something we have a lucky number called every so often and everyone having this number has a cigarette" (96th A.R.C. Archives).

In February 1945 the Red Cross workers decided to 'give their all' to give a show for the patients. Evelyn Edelson describes the show:

"Since our abilities were strictly limited to the contents of our footlockers, a style show was the order of the day. By combining all the odds and ends in two huts complete ensembles were assembled. The show consisted of various types of clothes 'straight from the U.S.A.' (at least two years old!) sports clothes, street clothes, formals, 'Time to retire' and 'full field pack' made up our wardrobes. The Special Service Officer acted as M.C. with an officer patient providing the background music as a pianist. ... Two performances were given and as much publicity had been given to 'The ARC is on Parade' standing room only prevailed at both shows. For weeks beforehand the Special Service Officer had interjected 'The ARC is on Parade' on the P.A. system at least six times every 30 minutes. ... We feel that our efforts were well worthwhile, as all the patients enjoyed our endeavours and appreciated it" (96th A.R.C. Archives).

In April the A.R.C. commenced a programme of redecoration and renovation for their buildings. The Recreation Hall was closed for two weeks while painters worked on the floor and walls. Drapes were made and hung. The girls also worked on the grounds around their building with the help of the men from the Rehabilitation ward. A 'patio' was laid which consisted of cement

Patients sitting on the new patio. (96th General Hospital Year Book).

blocks on the ground between the two tar paper huts. The huts were painted 'pink stucco', an effect produced by mixing plaster with paint. Turquoise blue flower boxes and doors completed the effect. Yellow wall flowers were planted in the flower boxes and sweet peas on a trellis on the back wall. A small round oak stained table was built to help camouflage the pipe in the centre of the patio. The girls also seeded a lawn and planted shrubs.

Sadly the girls did not have much chance to enjoy the new look of their building as plans had already been set into motion for their reassignment.

Chapter 7

A DIFFICULT AND IMPORTANT TASK

Towards the end of 1944 the hospital reverted back to its original function as a holding and evacuating unit. There was an increase in the number of cases arriving at the hospital that had already been put before a Disposition Board to decide on their return to the States. Very few cases arriving at the 96th at the end of 1944 were returned to duty.

This was thought to be due to an improvement in the work of other hospitals when dealing with combat cases. More potential neuropsychiatric combat cases had been screened and returned to duty from other hospitals so that it was no longer necessary for this type of patient to be treated at the 96th.

On April 12 1945 American servicemen and women in Britain received the sad news that the President of the United States and Commander in Chief of the U.S. Military Forces, Franklin D. Roosevelt, had died of a cerebral haemorrhage. Roosevelt had been President for 12 years and many Americans could not remember another President. He was a much loved leader and, as at other military bases, the flag was flown at half mast at Brickbarns to express the sorrow of the personnel. Tec.5 Frank T. Janik felt moved to write a piece of prose for the event. Sadly Roosevelt never saw V.E. Day which came less than a month after his death.

Following V.E. Day the patient census at Brickbarns gradually declined. In May 1945 evacuations exceeded admissions. As the 96th was the only neuropsychiatric general hospital available for redeployment it was informed that it would be reassigned to the Pacific Theatre of War.

The 312th Station Hospital was to take over the role that the 96th had been playing in England while the 130th General Hospital was to continue its role on the Continent. The 96th was ordered to hand over the hospital at Brickbarns to Detachment A of the 312th Station Hospital in July. Preparations for closure of the 96th General Hospital began in May.

In June Information and Education classes for all personnel became compulsory, even for the girls of the Red Cross unit. All personnel were also expected to practise drill. The Red Cross proudly noted that:

"When the nurses' platoon formed the Red Cross trained and drilled along with the nurses, many of whom were veterans in military drill. One day, when the platoon was given extra training, Miss Edelson outshone all the nurses and was acknowledged to be the sharpest member in a crack drill squad" (96th A.R.C. Archives).

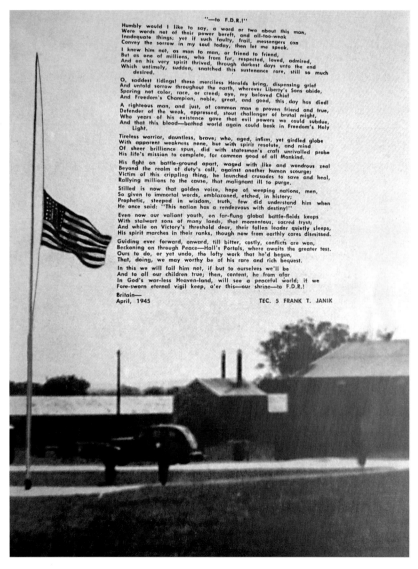

Flag flying at half mast for death of Roosevelt April 1945
(96th General Hospital Year Book).

In July Detachment A of the 312th arrived at Brickbarns and began taking over some of the responsibilities of the 96th. The two Red Cross units developed a working relationship to ensure that Red Cross work was carried out to satisfaction. At the beginning of July only about one eighth of the wards were open so the recreation programme was very limited. By the middle of July the complete Red Cross programme had been turned over to the 312th.

*Year Book produced by
96th General Hospital
(Authors' collection).*

There were some staff changes in the 96th at this point. There was to be a new Commanding Officer and Chief of N. P. Service. The new Table of Organisation required a unit of five Red Cross girls so it was decided that Miss Ellingson would not travel with the unit. On July 21 all the other girls had a complete physical examination. It was later decided to change the Recreation Worker and Secretary.

At the end of July there was a formal retreat and formal dinner held in honour of the Commanding Officer who had received orders for reassignment. In the Year Book which the 96th General Hospital produced Colonel Smith wrote:

"We have found a job here and I know have done it well. This is to us a great satisfaction." (96th General Hospital Year Book).

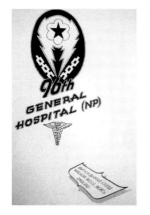
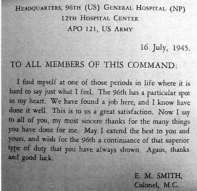

HEADQUARTERS, 96TH (US) GENERAL HOSPITAL (NP)
12TH HOSPITAL CENTER
APO 121, US ARMY

16 July, 1945.

TO ALL MEMBERS OF THIS COMMAND:

I find myself at one of those periods in life where it is hard to say just what I feel. The 96th has a particular spot in my heart. We have found a job here, and I know have done it well. This is to us a great satisfaction. Now I say to all of you, my most sincere thanks for the many things you have done for me. May I extend the best to you and yours, and wish for the 96th a continuance of that superior type of duty that you have always shown. Again, thanks and good luck.

E. M. SMITH,
Colonel, M.C.

*Left: Title page of 96th General Hospital Year Book.
Right: Piece written by Colonel Smith in 96th Year Book.*

In an article: 'the Ninety Sixth General Hospital' written in October 1946 Captain Henry Myers of the 96th reflects on the work carried out by the enlisted personnel and nurses of the 96th:

"Special mention is also merited for the nurses, ward men and Red Cross workers who were in daily contact with the patients and did so much to maintain and increase their morale. Unlike the medical officers there were relatively few transfers of nurse and ward men.

Most of them had to learn to deal with psychiatric patients without previous training. This they did with considerable therapeutic program which was aimed at putting every patient somewhere on the road to mental health even though a complete cure might not be possible in the time available. Efforts were made to have every patient understand his illness and feel that something was being done for him. While the program was not ideal ... the 96th General Hospital performed a difficult and important task and did it quietly and efficiently." (Ninety Sixth General Hospital – Henry Myers)

Detachment A of the 312th took over on August 4 and the 96th General Hospital remained in a staging status awaiting orders for direct redeployment. The end of the war in the Pacific brought orders for the personnel of the 96th to be discharged on their return to the U.S.

The 312th Station Hospital remained at Brickbarns until 31 August 1945 when it moved to Blandford, Dorset and was replaced by the 53rd General Hospital.

Nurse, Ann Serzo of the 96th General Hospital. (Cary Area Public Library).

FIGURE 11.—Col. Ernest H. Parsons, MC, Commanding Officer, 312th Station Hospital (NP), European Theater of Operations, U.S. Army.

(312th Station Hospital Archives).

Part Two:

Merebrook – Plant 4175

Chapter 8

CONVERTING BRICK BUILDINGS
INTO A HOSPITAL

The 53rd General Hospital arrived at Plant 4175, Merebrook Camp, on 5th March 1944. The personnel had travelled by train from Oulton Park, Cheshire, disembarking at Malvern Wells Station and marching to the site. An advance detachment of two officers: Captain Robert O'Sauer and Captain Fred W. Grahame and 52 enlisted men had arrived the day before by motor convoy and had prepared sleeping quarters and messing facilities for the arrival of the main body. The nurses joined the unit on the 6th March travelling from Manchester where they had been temporality assigned.

The site at Merebrook had originally been farmland. In 1942 it had been purchased by a factory owner from Birmingham who had little experience of farming. Godfrey Williams, who regularly helped out at the farm, remembers the arrival at the main entrance to the meadow of two large, highly polished cars. Seven men dressed in dark suits and carrying measuring tapes, marker pegs and hand mallets got out of the cars. Godfrey was surprised to see them measuring the land as the hay was not ready to be cut. When he approached the men he was told that the government had requisitioned thirty acres of the land to build a hospital.

The site would be occupied by the 53rd General Hospital which had been activated before the U.S. had declared war against the Axis forces, on 10th February 1941 at Fort Benning Georgia. It was established to train commissioned and enlisted personnel for the expected operation of a general hospital in the Communication Zone (U.K.) or Zone of the Interior (U.S.) in the event that the U.S.A. would become involved in the war that was raging in Europe. Shortly after its activation all personnel were transferred to the 21st and 24th General Hospitals. It was reactivated as the 53rd General Hospital on 15th July 1942.

Abram Wolowski was one of the men who was assigned to the 53rd as a Pfc. He had enlisted in the army in April 1942. When Abram enlisted the recruiter stated he would recommend his assignment to the meat cutting programme of the Quartermaster Corps as Abram had had previous experience in his father's butchers shop business. The fourth day after his induction he was sent to Camp Robinson, Arkansas for medical training and then sent to join the 53rd General Hospital at Fort Benning.

The daily routine at Fort Benning involved classroom lessons and field training. At the base hospital the men were assigned to various wards such as surgical, medical or orthopaedic. Abram was assigned to the operating room as a surgical technician.

In late December 1943 all those in the unit who were not already U.S. citizens were taken to the Supreme Court in Atlanta, Georgia, to be sworn in as citizens of the United States. Abram was a still a

Arnold Wallace
(A. Wallace).

Polish citizen at the time; he had travelled to America with his family from Poland in 1938. After he had been sworn in he was escorted to an area where a Master Sergeant was seated. He remembers:

"When my turn came the Master Sergeant, with a Southern drawl, asked for my name spelt slowly. I answered with Abram Wolowski. He interrupted me and 'suggested' that since I am now a U.S. citizen I should have a good American name. On the Sergeant's desk lay a copy of the 'Atlanta Journal' with a large headline that read: 'Henry Agar Wallace, Vice President of the United States. The 'W' in the V.P.'s name caught my eye and I asked the Sergeant if I could choose that name. He said 'yes' and asked for a first name. I chose Arnold Irving, the name of my cousin. As of that moment I became an American named 'Arnold Irving Wallace.'

Arnold was concerned about his family's reaction to the change of name and was worried that his brother, also in the U.S. Forces, would have a different surname to him. With the help of the chaplain at Fort Benning he was able to contact his brother by phone (the first time he had spoken to him for six months) and inform him of the name change. His brother was then able to change his name to George Wallace when he was sworn in as a U.S. citizen.

Just before Christmas 1943 the 53rd was moved to a staging area at Camp Kilmer, New Jersey. Nurse, Ruby Johnson remembers that it was so cold here that she struggled to practise gas mask drill by numbers. On 26th December the unit sailed on the Dutch ship, Christiaan Huygens. When the men of the 53rd boarded the boat they found their allotted area to be overcrowded as another unit was already on board. Fortunately the other unit was reassigned to another vessel. Although this left more room for the 53rd only half of the unit could be accommodated for eating and sleeping at one time so the men were divided into two groups, one group slept while the other group were above deck and vice versa. The nurses were boarded in bunk beds, six to a room in the state rooms that had been originally intended for two people.

As the ship sailed out of New York Harbour there was a life boat drill and all the personnel came on deck. Corpsman, Bob Garrison recalls:

"I will never forget how cold it was. I had on that heavy G.I. overcoat and still thought I would freeze to death."

Nurse Ruby Johnson (P. Williams).

After a couple of days at sea the ship moved into the Gulf Stream and Bob remembers that it felt much warmer. He also noticed with concern that the Christiaan Huygens was dropping behind the rest of the convoy. He and the other men were worried that the boat would become a sitting target for a U-boat attack. When the men were sent below that night the other ships could only just be seen on the distant horizon. The next morning when the men came on deck they saw with relief that they were back in the middle of the convoy.

M. S. Christiaan Huygens.

On the third day at sea Arnold Wallace remembers hearing explosions and was told that the accompanying destroyers were launching depth charges. He remembers that this continued for several days. Ruby Johnson remembers that one night the personnel were ordered to sleep with their clothes on in case of submarine attacks. She also recalls suffering from sea sickness on the crossing and not being able to keep anything down, not even crusts of dry bread. Unfortunately there was no medication available for seasickness.

On 9th January 1944 the ship docked in the Firth of Clyde in Scotland. At 0200 hours the next morning the unit debarked and entrained to the staging camp at Oulton Park, Cheshire. The camp was run by the 360th Engineer Regiment commanded by Colonel J.A Barksdale. It was also a temporary home to the 16th, 50th and 90th General Hospitals and the 232nd Station Hospital. (The 90th General Hospital was also destined to run one of the hospitals at Malvern)

On arrival at Oulton Park the motor officer ordered the vehicles for the use of the hospital. The unit received a Willy's jeep, four ¾ ton Dodge carriers, four ¾ ton Dodge ambulances, two British ¾ ton Austin ambulances, four 1½ ton Dodge personnel carriers (6 x 6) two 2½ ton GMC trucks, one Dennis Tipper, a Dodge fire truck and three trailers. A Wolseley Sedan was added to the Motor pool later and when the unit arrived at Merebrook it also had the use of a ¾ ton Dodge ambulance and a ¾ ton Austin ambulance belonging to the 12th Medical Centre. The advance party used the vehicles to travel in convoy from Oulton Park to Malvern.

At the end of February the nurses were sent to the 310th Station Hospital in Manchester for training and it was from here that they travelled to Merebrook on 6th March.

When the unit arrived at Merebrook the site was still incomplete. Richard Lloyd, from Danemoor Farm remembers seeing the camp in its various stages of construction as he had to walk past it on his way to school. He recalls watching the Irish navvies carrying out the construction and remembers thinking that they were making slow progress.

Upon the arrival of the 53rd eleven huts in the enlisted area were still being used to house the civilian labourers. This led to the temporary overcrowding of the enlisted men in the remaining nissen huts. Only half of the wards were completed and it was necessary to use the enlisted mess for the entire staff for the first three weeks. A combined officers and nurses mess was opened on 7th March. The patients mess was opened on 24th April and a separate mess for officer patients on 26th June.

The Commanding officer, Colonel Wayne Brandstadt describes his first impressions of the site in the archives for the 53rd:

"Upon arrival at this installation, soon after the first of March 1944, the buildings were thought to be in an advanced stage of construction but still requiring all the minor adjustments that would convert it from a set of brick buildings into a hospital. This included such things as installation of sterilising units, electrical outlets, reconversion of current to adapt it to American equipment, the installation of two large special tubs in the burn ward, physiotherapy equipment and particularly the special problems relating to the operating room such as water distillers and operating lights" (53rd General Hospital Archives).

Nurses living quarters at Oulton Park (Judy Brinkman).

Top left: Motor Pool at 53rd General Hospital (53rd General Hospital Archives).
Top right: Malvern Hills (Judy Brinkman). Centre and Bottom: Photographs of
hospital with Malvern Hills in background (Judy Brinkman).

Aerial view of Merebrook (English Heritage).

Arnold Wallace describes his first impressions of the site:

"It was a single floor structure with a central building and a number of corridors like an octopus with many tentacles. Each wing was designed for a single speciality: surgical wing, medical wing, orthopaedic wing etc. The central building served as an administration centre, records and doctors offices. One wing contained Operating Rooms and these were well planned by the British. As well as a Rehab Wing, the Motor Pool, Kitchen, sleeping quarters, laundry and other facilities were outside the main hospital. It was like a small self contained city."

Arnold felt optimistic on his arrival:

"My first recollection was one of pleasant response. My thoughts of being overseas in a war zone were quickly eased by noting the completed facilities, the relative quiet of the surrounding civilian populace and the immediate involvement of our officers and non-coms in getting us involved in setting up our own specialised areas."

Mess Building (Judy Brinkman).

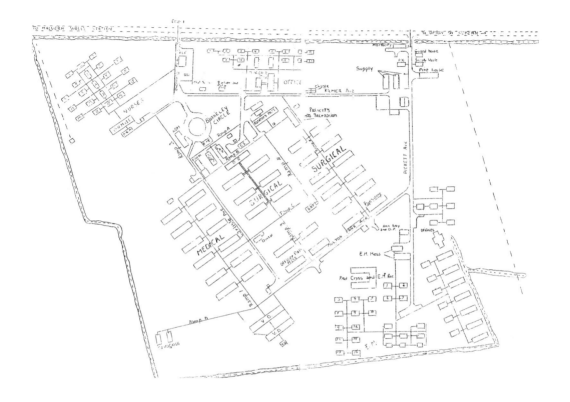

Plan of Merebrook Camp (53rd General Hospital Archives).

The unit spent until 24th April preparing the hospital site and undergoing training. Arnold remembers;

"We were restricted to camp for about a week with numerous lectures concerning our behaviour in the camp and outside the camp area. The topics that were covered in lectures involved the history of the area, type of civilian population, types of available recreation and interpersonal relations with Allied hosts. Eventually passes were issued to staff on a rotating basis. Army trucks took us into town and returned us back to camp around 10.00p.m."

As each building was finished the British turned it over to the 53rd. Each section could then begin to construct fixtures and fittings for their buildings. Shelves, cupboards, tables, benches, files and boxes of various kinds were constructed. Bob Garrison, who was assigned to the pharmacy, remembers unpacking the drugs and equipment under the watchful eye of the Chief of Pharmacy, Tech Sgt Sidney Berber. He remembers that the pharmacy was well equipped. Bob's duties were to make up capsules and solutions to be dispensed. He remembers making thousands of APC capsules and five gallon jugs of terpin hydrate cough syrup. Ruby Johnson remembers that the personnel at the pharmacy were also expert at making a delicious cordial from blackberries that she and other nurses picked from the hedgerows.

Top: Arnold Wallace (standing, 3rd from right) with colleagues outside hut. (Arnold Wallace). Bottom left: Preparing the hospital grounds (Judy Brinkman) Bottom right: Commanding Officer of the 53rd General Hospital, Lieutenant Colonel Wayne G. Brandstadt (53rd General Hospital Year Book).

Bob Garrison and colleagues outside huts (53rd General Hospital Year Book).

The utility section constructed an arch for the main gate and made bicycle racks for all areas of the grounds as well as litter racks, fire point racks and mail racks for each ward.

On 21st April 1944 a formal retreat was held at the camp and the American flag was raised for the first time on the post. At midnight following this ceremony the hospital was officially opened to receive patients. On 24th April the first patient, Sergeant Worth C. Wagner, Battery A, 3rd Field Artillery Observation Battalion was admitted. By 26th April all wards, operating rooms, laboratories and clinics were fully equipped and ready to operate. Initially there were some shortages of equipment which were reported to the Chief Surgeon, ETOUSA and assemblage was finally completed on 1st July 1944.

The hospital was designated a Z.I. hospital so 170 patients from the 19th General Hospital due to be transferred to the Zone of Interior were also admitted on 24th April. The 53rd were told that their specific mission was:

" ... *the conservation of man power and the rapid evacuation of non-effectives"* (*53rd General Hospital Archives*).

On admission to the 53rd each patient's condition was evaluated and those whom it was believed would not be ready for general or limited duty within 180 days of the date of admission were brought before a board for return to the Zone of Interior for further treatment. This would make more room for more patients who could be treated and sent back to duty.

At the height of the conflict in Europe the bed situation in hospitals became critical and the number of days was reduced to 120 days so that a larger number of patients could be sent back to the States, thus releasing more beds for fresh patients. Later on a sixty day hospitalisation rule was brought in for a short time.

As well as being a Z.I. Hospital the 53rd was designated to heal burns, maxillofacial injuries and carry out plastic surgery for patients within the 12th Hospital Centre. The 53rd also served as a station hospital and out patients clinic for nearby units such as the G24 depot at Honeybourne and the G25 depot at Ashchurch, the 553 and 602 Engineer Battalions, 347 and 1310 Engineer Regiments, 411, 414 and 519 AAA Gun Battalions, 182 Field Artillery Group and the 970 Engineer Maintenance Company.

Main Gate September 1944 (53rd General Hospital Archives).

Top: Entrance to 53rd General Hospital (53rd General Hospital Year Book).
Bottom left: Laboratory at the 53rd General Hospital (53rd General Hospital
archives. Bottom right: American flag flying on the post (J. Brinkman).

Chapter 9

'HOMINUM CAUSA'

O n 26th May 1944 the 53rd General Hospital started preparing for the arrival of wounded combat soldiers from the Normandy invasion. On 6th June 29 ward tents were erected on the ends of wards and extra equipment and supplies were distributed. On 10th June the hospital was informed that the arrival of a large number of casualties was imminent and a few hours later the first train load of over 200 casualties arrived. One of the patients would be the first casualty from the invasion to reach the Z.I. Bob Garrison remembers that as the patients arrived:

"The whole hospital turned out to become litter bearers and rank did not make any difference."

The author of the 53rd General Hospital Year Book (distributed to the personnel of the 53rd at the end of the war) describes the impact of the arrival of battle casualties on the unit:

Emblem of the 53rd General Hospital (53rd General Hospital Year Book).

"The first real test came with the first trainload of battle casualties following the invasion of the European continent. Everyone did a good job. The sight of these battle casualties brought a full realisation of the effects of the present day welfare. The heart and soul of every man and woman was in the work to be done. The patients were given the best possible care and treatment to be had. The wounded soldiers, exhausted but uncomplaining were received, put to bed, given urgent treatment and most important of all, rest and food. All in record time. This was indeed an achievement for the manner and time in which all was

Photo of patient at the 53rd. Ward tents can be seen in the background. (J. Brinkman).

accomplished reflected earnest effort and success of early training. Within a matter of a few hours all was quiet and peaceful again" (53rd General Hospital Year Book).

Arnold Wallace reflects on his reaction to the arrival of the wounded on that day.

"On that day the whole world changed, even my rank to Corporal. ... We trained and were prepared for the day physically but not so well mentally."

Arnold recalls that at first the personnel of the 53rd felt some relief when they heard the news of the D-Day assault on the morning of June 6th. They awaited the casualties with anticipation. When the patients arrived there was a different reaction. Arnold writes:

"What a shock to see young kids my age, eighteen, nineteen and plus with severe bullet, shrapnel and concussion wounds and in addition non-physical wounds, shell shocked, mentally, in a stupor or hysterical. No matter how much we had prepared for this it still left a lump in your throat and an ache in your heart. Amazingly the 53rd quickly applied their training and their individual skills to ease the physical and mental pain of the wounded. We had six O.R surgical stations filled with doctors, nurses and surgical technicians. Our entire focus now was to do our job and we did it well."

The surgical department found this first train load of patients to be generally in a worse state than those who arrived on later trains:

"With the first influx of battle casualties were many cases whose general condition was worse than that seen in subsequent groups. Their wounds were not as clean and less thoroughly debrided and the patients were generally more exhausted. One might attribute this to the chaotic state of the beachheads immediately following invasion. Subsequent trainloads discharged casualties which in contrast presented excellently debrided wounds, which in most cases were free of infection. Their general condition was excellence and few cases required shock treatment, transfusions or intravenous fluid. With the establishment of general hospitals on the continent the number of early

evacuees became less numerous and casualties arrived here from 7-14 days after being wounded. Most cases treated in the surgical section were fragmental wounds of the upper and lower extremities" (53rd General Hospital Archives).

Within a few days of the arrival of the first train load the hospital was full to capacity. The girls of the Red Cross unit met the trains, taking cigarettes and gum to distribute to the patients. One staff member rode back to the hospital with each busload of ambulatory cases to guide them to their destination within the hospitals. Usually patients would be admitted directly to their wards but on one occasion in June there was a larger group of ambulatory patients than had been expected so two of the Red Cross girls opened the Assembly Hall at 2.00a.m. and served coffee, cake and sandwiches from the Mess Hall to the men while they waited for ward assignments.

Most of the patients arrived without their belongings. The Quartermaster Supply Department at the post issued the men with new uniforms where necessary. From April to December 1944 it was necessary to issue 4385 patients with a full allowance of clothing and equipment. Other patients needed only to be issued with shoes, socks or mess equipment. The Red Cross supplied comfort articles such as toiletries and razors although they found their initial supply was almost entirely used up on the first trainload of patients. When the stock was exhausted it was necessary to use Red Cross funds to buy articles from the P.X. for the men. During June 1944 the girls spent £285.15s. 4d at the P.X. on behalf of the patients.

The Red Cross also provided loans for the men who arrived at the hospital with no money at all. Some of the patients had a few notes of invasion money but the hospital authorities were unable to exchange the

Left: Ambulances collecting casualties from the Malvern Wells G.W.R. Station (J. Brinkman). Right: Ambulances line up at Merebrook (J. Brinkman).

French money until about a fortnight after the arrival of the first train. In an effort to get the loans as soon as possible the girls placed mimeographed forms on the wards for the patients to fill in. Demand was so great that the loan forms quickly ran out.

With the large influx of surgical patients at Merebrook after D-Day the Medical Section was called upon to assist the surgical section of the hospital. For a time after D-Day the medical section took up only two wards in the hospital which were supervised by the Chief of the Medical Service.

Arnold Wallace recalls that after the initial surge of wounded a routine was established in the hospital and there was a sense of:

"... *normality – whilst initially my mind was on my job I now began to think and worry about my brother, George ... Around the second week in November a*

Top: Train carrying patients for 53rd General Hospital at Malvern Wells L.M.S. Station July 1944 (53rd General Hospital Archives). Bottom: Waiting for trains carrying patients for the 53rd (J. Brinkman).

sergeant from the Ambulance Corps came to see me. He had brought a convoy of new casualties and told me that one of the wounded claimed to be my brother."

Arnold went to the surgical ward where he found his brother sitting on a bed with a wrist injury. He discovered that George had been in Belgium pushing towards Germany with the 104th Division when he had been injured in the wrist during a German counter attack with heavy shelling. He had dressed his own wound with the bandage and sulphanilamide powder in his first aid canister on his pistol belt and remained with the platoon. The following day the company medic redressed the wound and instructed George to report to the Field Aid Station. Discolouration and swelling was evident around the wound so the Field Officer ordered George to report for transfer to a general

Patients at the 53rd (J. Brinkman).

hospital. At the transfer location George requested a transfer to the 53rd General Hospital where his brother was assigned.

When Major Feingold, the officer in charge of Arnold's section, learnt that Arnold's brother had been admitted he made a point of seeing George and determining the diagnosis of gas gangrene. The swelling and discolouration was due to a type of bacteria which forms gases in the muscle tissue. After incising and draining the wound it could be treated with the new antibiotic, penicillin.

The Major allowed Arnold to aid in the surgical procedure on his brother's wrist. After the surgery a bottle of penicillin solution was set up to drip into the operative area. After a few days of the drip procedure the swelling receded and the colour returned to normal. Finally the wound was treated with penicillin ointment. Arnold writes:

"I know that the new antibiotic treatment and Major Feingold's surgical skill saved my brothers arm."

A month after surgery Major Feingold put George in a rehabilitation programme to restore proper use and strength to the arm. In mid January he was transferred to a Replacement Depot where he was assigned as a driver delivering trucks to France. Once the truck was delivered George would return to England to pick up a new truck. In between trips George was able to get a pass so that he could visit his brother.

Another patient who was reunited with his brother at Merebrook was Al Lombino. Al had been drafted in 1942 and had been trained as a medic. After ten weeks he was transferred to a hospital for veterans. He didn't enjoy that assignment so he transferred to M.P. Duty. In March 1943 he volunteered for combat duty and was given orders to go overseas. He boarded a captured German ship in New York Harbour and set sail. One night when on guard duty he remembers feeling very cold so he asked one of the sailors the ship's location. The sailor told Al that they were just off the coast of Newfoundland heading for England. Al was surprised as he had just undergone jungle warfare training in the U.S. and was wearing a summer Khaki uniform that was designed for the Pacific. The ship sailed into the Firth of Clyde in Scotland but it was necessary to wait until the next morning to dock as the harbour was protected by anti submarine chains. From Scotland Al travelled by train to London, the train stopping from time to time because of air raids.

Around the middle of July 1944 Al boarded an Indian ship to sail to Omaha Beach which he remembers was still very busy, a month after D-Day. He and the others marched to St. Lo where they found that they were to be replacements for Company K, 175 Regiment, 29th infantry Division, which had been hard hit on D-Day. Al was assigned a rifle with an adapter for firing grenades which acted as an anti-tank weapon.

The 29th did not encounter much opposition until they arrived in St. Lo where Al remembers:

"All hell broke loose for a day or so."

February 1945. George and Arnold Wallace. George was on a visit to Arnold after his reassignment (A. Wallace).

Right: Al Lombino (A. Lombino).

The 29th regrouped and received more replacements while the Ninth Air Force flew low over St. Lo hitting German gun emplacements, thus enabling the troops to break out of the city. On 28th July the men packed and prepared to move. Al remembers that for the first time since his arrival in France he was able to ride in a truck. At one point on the drive out of St. Lo it was necessary for the trucks to move off the road so that a division of tanks could get by as they moved forward to support infantry units on the front lines.

On 29th July Al was in combat, he remembers running behind another G.I. in crouch position when he was hit in both of his legs. He remembers very little from that moment until he awoke on a beach facing the doors of a Landing Ship Tank. He does remember coming to in a tented field hospital prior to this, where a doctor asked if he could wear Al's field jacket to keep out the cold. The Landing Ship Tank transported Al across the Channel to England. LST's were the largest vessels that could land vehicles and men directly on to the beaches. After D-Day some were equipped as hospital ships and had brackets mounted in the bulkheads to support stretchers. A large number of casualties could be transported in this way as stretchers could fill the floor of the tank deck as well as the bulkheads. When Al woke again he was on a train having a blood transfusion. The next time he regained consciousness he found himself at the 53rd General Hospital. Al drifted in and out of consciousness until the first week in September.

At the 53rd Al was put on a critical list. He had been hit in a main artery on his left leg at the back of his knee and he had lost a large amount of blood from both legs. Gangrene had set in and it was necessarily to amputate part of one foot. As Al had no feeling in either of his legs Major Feingold intended to amputate the ball of his foot with no anaesthesia.

Left: L-R. Arnold Wallace, Chaplain, Al Lombino and another patient in front of Ward 15. (A. Wallace). Right: Al Lombino, back in the United States Easter 1945. (A. Lombino).

Film boxes containing colour cine-film of the 53rd General Hospital belonging to chief Nurse, Verla Thompson.

After the amputation Al began to make a slow recovery although one of his legs could not be saved and when he returned to the U.S. it was necessary to amputate the leg below the left knee. Because of the condition of his legs Al was confined to the ward until December when he was sent back to the U.S.

While at the 53rd, Al was pleased to discover that two of the personnel on his ward, Major Feingold and Sergeant Arnold Wallace, came from his home town of Brooklyn, New York. Al recalls that each morning Arnold would wake up the patients on the ward and prepare them for breakfast. Al remembers that he rarely got much sleep at the 53rd. Each night, shortly after lights out, he would hear the drone of RAF planes flying over the hospital towards Germany. He and his fellow patients would attempt to count how many flew over and then a few hours later count the number returning.

On one occasion Arnold Wallace helped Al out of bed to have his picture taken outside of the ward. Arnold took the photos to the Photo Lab at the hospital to be developed. In April 1944 the Special Service at the 53rd had set up a photo shop on the post where the personnel could have films developed and prints made. (Special Service also commenced work on a photo yearbook which was to contain photos of the personnel and the camp. This was published the following year.) Al was sent back to the U.S. before the photos were developed and he didn't get to see the photo until 2008 when he contacted the authors who also put him back in contact with Arnold Wallace.

One morning when lying in the ward with the sheet over his head Al felt someone touching his feet. Thinking that it was Arnold playing a joke Al threw back the sheet to throw a punch at him. To his surprise he saw that it was his older brother, Lenny, who immediately started scolding him for volunteering for combat duty when he could have been a medic.

Lenny was with the 17th Base Post Office, working alongside the 1st Base Post Office at the time. He was based in Sutton Coldfield near Birmingham. The 1st Base Post Office dealt with all the mail for G.I.s in the European Theatre of Operations and was responsible for redirecting mail for wounded soldiers assigned to hospitals or sent home. The 17th Base Post Office, known as the Invasion Post Office, worked alongside the 1st Base Post Office until their post office could be set up in France to deal with mail for the invasion forces. Because Lenny worked with the redirected mail he was able to find his brother's location. He couldn't get a pass so he went AWOL to visit his brother.

While visiting Al, Lenny took the names of all the patients on the ward so that he could personally speed up the redirection process and ensure that they would receive the mail promptly. In fact Al recalls that the hospital was flooded with mail and packages after Lenny's visit. Al remembers receiving some sweets that had gone hard and white with age and although he was meant to be on a 'light food intake' he recalls that:

"It sure was a good treat."

Strangely, while Al had been awaiting shipment to France in July prior to his injury and hospitalisation, he had been sitting on the driver's side of a 2½ ton truck when he heard his surname called. The men who called him were part of an advance party of the 17th B.P.O. and had mistaken Al for his brother, Lenny, who was still in Sutton Coldfield at this point.

When Lenny moved to France the nurses on Al's ward sent him packets of Camel cigarettes in exchange for French perfume. Al remembers the ward smelling strongly of violets at this time.

One day, while in France, a colleague offered to pay Lenny $20, if he would stand in for him to take the mail by plane to forward units in Belgium. Lenny agreed but when he opened the door of the plane to distribute the mail an officer ordered him to:

"Step down soldier; we need you at the Bulge."

Lenny protested that he was serving with the mail service but the officer's reply was:

"You are now in the infantry."

Lenny had no choice but to obey.

Two weeks later another mail plane arrived from Paris. When the door opened he saw his colleague who with surprise, asked him what he was doing as he had been reported AWOL. By this time Lenny had frost bitten feet and was very cold as he had no change of winter clothes with him. He travelled back on the plane to rejoin his unit in Paris where he attempted to explain what had happened to his Commanding Officer whose retort was:

"That's a likely story. Who's the girl?!"

As the weather worsened on the continent the 53rd received a large number of trench foot patients. Over 300 cases of trench foot were admitted during November and December 1944. Colonel Brandstadt wrote:

"These and an increase in upper respiratory disease and combat exhaustion account for the increase in … medical cases. Most of the patients have been received as transfers from other general hospitals nearer the actual scene of fighting. This has resulted in a group that by and large cannot be fit for further duty in this theatre within the period allowed for treatment" (53rd Archives).

Elaine Wakefield, the Assistant Field Director of the Red Cross wrote:

"We were swarmed with hundreds of restless and anxious ambulatory patients. We realised that a very active and varied program with many off-post activities was imperative as passes were denied these men in case of sudden alertments. We found the military most cooperative and interested in assisting us whenever possible in scheduling a variety of activities for the patients. When sudden alertments were not in view we were permitted to carry on off-post activities. Our Commanding Officer agreed to picnics, home hospitality tours and dances off the post under Red Cross supervision and sponsorship" (ARC 53).

By December 1944 it was necessary to expand the facilities at the hospital. On 10th December a 160 bed expansion unit was requisitioned. On 30th December peak load was reached when the hospital had 1512 patients (The normal capacity for a General Hospital was 1084).

Some of the patients received at the hospital could be sent to other hospitals with specialisms in the area. Those with peripheral nerve injuries and head injuries could be transferred to the neurosurgical centre at Wood Farm once wounds had been cleansed and closed secondarily. Patients with chest injuries were transferred to the Thoracic Centre at Blackmore Park. Patients from the other Malvern Hospitals needing plastic surgery were sent to Merebrook.

The Plastic Surgery Section of the Surgical Service was particularly busy. From 10th June onwards the section received so many patients that it was impossible for the personnel within the section to carry out all the work. Other surgical personnel were taught to carry out the routine of skin grafts. During June to December 1944 63 burn patients were received at the hospital. Malcolm Mason, a civilian worker at Wood Farm remembers on one occasion a soldier brought in by air whose flesh was raw because he had been hit with a flame thrower. Some of the burn patients had been carelessly burnt from the improper handling of gasoline field stoves.

A number of patients with facial injuries had been blinded. After treatment these men were sent to St. Dunstan's (charity for blind servicemen) for preliminary training prior to being sent to the Zone of the Interior. Colonel Brandstadt described these patients in his report for 1944:

"Their adjustment to their handicap has been a morale boosting factor for the less severely injured eye patients" (53rd archives).

Enucleations were provided with glass ball implants in most cases. Acrylic prostheses were made by the prosthedentist.

James Coleman (M. Stateler).

In July 1945 Private James M. Coleman was transferred to the 53rd General Hospital from the 182nd General Hospital in Derbyshire so that a prosthetic eye could be made for him. James had been serving with the 505th Parachute Infantry Regiment, 82nd Airborne Division in operation Market Garden when, he was blinded in the left eye. He had previously completed combat jumps in Sicily, Italy and Normandy without incident although he had nearly missed the Normandy jump as he had taken unauthorised leave to visit a girlfriend even though all military personnel were confined to barracks on the period running up to D-Day.

On 17th September 1944 James' unit was dropped into the Nijmegen Grave region of Holland. The unit took the Maas Bridge at Grave, the Maastraal Canal Bridge at Heumen and the Nijmegen – Groesbeek Ridge but attempts to take Nijmegen Highway Bridge failed.

On September 19th the unit was pinned down and unable to advance because of fire from enemy automatic weapons. With little thought for his own safety James crawled forward under a barrage of artillery, mortars and machine gun fire to locate the enemy weapons, deliberately exposing himself to draw fire. He was hit by enemy machine gun fire in both hands and the left eye but managed to return to his unit with the information needed to destroy the enemy gun positions. He was awarded the Bronze Star Medal for Heroic Conduct.

From Holland James was sent to the 86th British General Hospital in Belgium where his left eye was removed on 28th September. From here he was evacuated to the 61st General Hospital at Burford until November 1944

Press photograph of factory tour in Nottingham. James Coleman is seated far right wearing eye patch (M. Stateler).

where, due to an error in his paperwork, he was sent back to duty for 2 weeks. He was then sent to the 182nd General Hospital in Sudbury Derbyshire for reclassification until February 1945. While at the 182nd he was taken for a tour through a war plant at Nottingham where press pictures of him were taken. Meanwhile James's mother had contacted the Red Cross to find the whereabouts of her son as he had not written home for a while. The Red Cross located him and sent his mother the pictures taken at the factory which showed him wearing an eye patch. This is how she found out he had lost an eye; James had not contacted her earlier as he did not want her to worry about his injury.

From February to June 1945 James was assigned to limited duty and then sent to the 53rd General Hospital for an eye prosthesis for his left eye socket. Unfortunately by this time the dental officer who made prosthesis had been transferred back to the Zone of Inferior so at the end of July James was evacuated to the U.S. for the eye to be made and fitted.

Paperwork regarding James Coleman's injuries from
53rd General Hospital. (M. Stateler).

Chapter 10

NOT ALL WORK AND NO PLAY

Upon the arrival of the nurses at Merebrook arrangements were made for the expected large influx of patients. One of the empty wards was turned into a workshop and swabs, dressings and other sterile supplies were made and prepared in readiness for the rush after D-Day. Because of the large number of patients arriving at the hospital from 10th June onwards there was a shortage of some supplies. Nurses cut up their own towels to make face clothes for the patients and shared their own cigarette rations with them. Colonel Brandstadt praises the nurses in his report for doing:

" … more than their share of work" (53rd General Hospital Archives).

At the end of 1944 he commented that they had:

" … become proficient in the care of dressing and serving the needs of the sick. At the same time they have kept the wards neat and clean at all times. Beyond that they have maintained the necessary degree of discipline and at the same time have been the most important single factor in the morale of these wounded men" (53rd General Hospital Archives).

However, shortly after the arrival of the 53rd at Merebrook there was some dissatisfaction amongst the nurses, so much so that one wrote a six page letter to her Congressman complaining about the conditions at Merebrook. The Congressman, Earle D. Witley, passed on the information to the Army Nurse Corps Director, Lieutenant Colonel Ida Danielson, commenting:

"Ordinary humanity, however, may permit me to say that if 50% of the statements are accurate then the women of the Army Nurse Corps have endured unnecessary exposure to the rain, the cold and to unreasonable and administrative eccentricities that are a positive disgrace to that administration" (53rd General Hospital Archives).

He goes on to complain that several nurses had been rendered physically unfit for service because of the conditions they were working under and to state that:

"It truly seems that these women have endured more hardship already that I did during my thirteen months in the AEF although I was at the front" (53rd General Hospital Archives).

Left: Nurse Ruby Johnson and two patients (P. Williams).
Right: Nurse helping patients (J. Brinkman).

Lieutenant Colonel Danielson passed this information onto Major Agnes Resch, Chief Nurse of the 12th Hospital Center, and she spoke to Colonel Brandstadt and Captain Verla Thompson, Chief Nurse of the 53rd. Major Resch reported back:

"It is not believed that there were any unreasonable administrative eccentricities. As part of an established training programme the nurses of a unit waiting for patients have a certain amount of outdoor and physical training and exercise and also help to get the wards ready for occupancy. No doubt the temporary lack of professional work causes some of the nurses to get disheartened and want to complain but it is my opinion that the morale of most of the nurses of the 53rd General Hospital is very high" (53rd General Hospital Archives).

Major Resch goes onto mention that only ten nurses had reported sick in the period March to April and that only six of these had upper respiratory infections which may have been due to the change in climate.

The matter appears to have been dropped at this point through lack of evidence but Nurse Ruby Johnson, whose sister, Dixie, also served with the 53rd, describes her barracks as being cold and damp:

"My living quarters were a Nissen hut, which was shared by six other nurses. The bunks had no sheets, just woollen blankets. The mattresses were in three pieces and we never figured out why. A pot belly stove in the corner of the barracks furnished our heat. The floor was bare cement. There was a coal pile near and we carried our own supply as needed. A British maid swept the floor and removed the ashes. No clothes closet, just a shelf and rod for hanging our clothes. The climate was very damp and we experienced mould in our shoes. Laundry was done either in a sink or bath tub. My personal items and wool nurse uniforms I washed by hand. Our uniforms for work were brown and white striped seersucker. Our dress uniforms were olive drab. Lingerie was also olive drab. Shoes were brown. Fatigue uniforms were coveralls and WAC boots."

In a transcribed interview Chief Nurse, Verla Thompson recounts the time that there was a complaint about two of the 53rd nurses who had passes to travel to London. They had been seen wearing their O.D. nurse dresses off post when they should have been wearing a jacket and skirt. When she questioned the two girls they explained that they had taken their dresses in their suitcases to wear at an office club in London, which they were allowed to do. In the interview Verla admits that she didn't enjoy reprimanding the girls but she accepted it as part of her job.

HEADQUARTERS, 12TH (US) MEDICAL HOSPITAL CENTER
Office of the Chief Nurse
APO 121, U. S. Army

10 August 1944

Ida W. Danielson
Lt. Col. A.N.C. Director
Office of the Chief Surgeon
COM Z, ETOUSA, APO 871, U.S. Army

My dear Col. Danielson:

Yesterday, I received the extract which you sent me from Congressman Earle D. Willey's letter.

Information obtained from the Commanding Officer, Lt. Colonel Brandstadt and the Chief Nurse, Captain Thompson of the 53rd General Hospital shows that from the time this hospital arrived at its present site (quoted in Congressman Willey's letter) on 6th March until the hospital received patients on 24th April, that 10 Nurses reported sick. Only 6 of these were upper respiratory infections and might have been due to changes in climate. None of these was very ill.

It is not believed that there were any unreasonable administrative eccentricities. As a part of an established training program, the nurses of a unit waiting for patients have a certain amount of outdoor physical training and exercise, and also help to get the wards ready for occupancy. No doubt the temporary lack of professional work caused some of the nurses to get disheartened and want to complain but it is my opinion that the morale of most of the nurses at the 53rd General Hospital is very high.

Both the Commanding Officer and the Chief Nurse are interested in the welfare of their nurses and can offer no suggestion as to which nurse might have written to Congressman Willey.

Sincerely,

AGNES A. RESCH
Major, A.N.C.
Asst. Supt.

Letter sent to Lt Col. Ida Danielson from Major Agnes Resch (J. Brinkman).

Top: Nurses' Living quarters (J. Brinkman). Bottom left: Dixie Johnson (P. Williams). Bottom right: Some of the nurses of the 53rd. Ruby Johnson and Dixie Johnson are standing at each end of the line. (P. Williams)

Ruby Johnson remembers that the nurses were allowed very little time off duty because the hospital was so busy. She recalls that by the time she was discharged she had accrued 45 days leave. However she also comments that:

"All was not work and no play. Frequently we went to pubs and pitched darts. Usually the English won."

She only remembers one occasion when she pitched the winning dart in a game against an English team. She also recalls visits to the Officers Club on base where the officers and nurses could relax and play cards.

A large number of the detachment personnel spent some time in the pubs in the vicinity of the hospital. Peggy Webb, who was in the Land Army at the time, remembers G.I.S. from Merebrook visiting the Swan and The Ewe and Lamb. She recalls that often patients with their arms in casts would visit The

Chief Nurse, Verla Thompson and Assistant Chief Nurse Captain Bertha E. Thornhill (53rd General Hospital Year Book).

Ewe and Lamb. As they were not supposed to be off base they would pay some of the local children to look out for MPs. She also remembers that the dog at the pub had a litter of pups and one of the detachment personnel took one of the pups to keep him company on guard duty.

Ben Sliwinski, who was a pharmacist's assistant at the 53rd, recalls a dog at one of the pubs he visited. He remembers that the dog would befriend all who entered the place but at closing time when they bartender shouted '*Time*'

M.P.s from the 53rd General Hospital (53rd General Hospital Year Book).

the dog would immediately run around the room barking at the patrons and nipping their ankles. Bob Garrison, also a pharmacist assistant at the 53rd remembers that whiskey would be served in pubs until 9.00p.m. After that he and his colleagues would drink sherry wine and chase it with beer.

Ben also remembers arriving at the pub with a group of colleagues on one occasion to find that there was a broken window in the front of the building, fearing that the group might be blamed for the incident the men took up a collection to pay for a replacement window. Although the men didn't believe that anyone in their group was responsible for the damage it was agreed paying for a new window might strengthen Anglo-American relationships.

The personnel of the 53rd also enjoyed visiting the dances at the Winter Gardens in Malvern where they could meet British girls. Nineteen year old Arnold Wallace remembers:

"The young ladies were, from my young frame of reference, courteous, pretty, interesting conversationalists and eager to learn about us Americans. This relationship made the loneliness of being thousands of miles from home and the nearness of the warzone more secure ...

Bob Garrison.
(R. Garrison).

Back in camp we would compare the mental and physical qualities of the young ladies we met. After several visitations to U.S.O. dances we started to pair up with young ladies who became our dance partners. One such lady became my dance partner. When I first met her and asked her for her name she replied: 'Betty'. 'Betty what?' I asked. 'Betty Davis' she replied. I looked at her with a smile and said: 'Yeah, sure, and my name is Clarke Gable'. We had a good laugh and she became my favourite date."

Arnold remembers that one rainy night he and his colleague, George Eliopoulos, missed their transportation back to the camp because they had escorted their dates home. They decided to walk but were soon wet through, so they took shelter in an open barn they passed. They made themselves comfortable in the hay and soon fell asleep. When they awoke several hours later it was dry so they prepared to continue their walk back to camp. As Arnold got up he tripped over something under the hay. Upon examination he found it to be a motorbike.

As the men started to walk back to camp one of their ambulances passed them and gave them a lift. Fortunately they were not punished for being late back as they got back before reveille when roll call was taken.

The next time the two men went into town they visited the owner of the barn and arranged to buy the 1920's Royal Enfield for £10 even though it was not in running order. When they returned to camp Arnold asked a friend in the Motor Pool to take a look at the bike. In two weeks the mechanic had the bike running but warned Arnold to be careful as the brakes were not very reliable. He also showed Arnold how to light the front 'alcohol lamp' with a match.

Arnold rode the bike around camp for a while and then applied for a permit to ride it on the road. When he and George had a day's pass they made plans to visit Birmingham. After riding for ten miles the brakes failed and the bike narrowly missed colliding with a large truck. At that point the men decided to return to camp where the mechanic made adjustments to the brakes and advised them to forget about trips outside the camp. Any future trips off the base were made by truck or train.

Arnold did get the chance to travel to Glasgow, Scotland, on a three day pass to visit his aunt. When his aunt came into wake him on the first morning she informed him of the sad news of the death of President Roosevelt.

On the day that Roosevelt died Bob Garrison recalls that he was off base in Great Malvern. He remembers that a number of local people approached him to express their sorrow at Roosevelt's death.

As well as the American personnel based at Merebrook there were a number of British civilian workers. By the time the hospital opened for patients in April

1944 there were five British civilians assigned who had been secured through the Ministry of Labour. By 31st December there were 37 working at the plant. Most of the posts were connected to the maintenance of the plant and technical duties such as telephone switchboard operators and stenographs.

Jim Appleby was one of the civilian workers at Merebrook. He had suffered in a gas attack in World War I and could only carry out light duties such as cooking and cleaning. The staff in the cook house would often give him left over portions of food. These were much bigger portions that he was accustomed to in a time of rationing. Jim's niece Jan Green remembers how shocked Jim was that in the mess building the white G.I.s sat at the tables while the black G.I.s ate standing up around the walls. Jim often worked in the neuropsychiatric ward and would sometimes invite two or three of the patients to tea, much to the annoyance of his wife.

In the period from 24th April to 11th June the neuropsychiatric section worked in a consulting capacity to both medical and surgical services. From 11th June, after the first train load of combat casualties, it was necessary to open a ward purely for neuropsychiatric patients. By 18th June there were nearly 90 neuropsychiatric patients; the peak load for the year was 190. Psychoneurosis anxiety state was the most frequent diagnosis. The majority of the cases were acute although most had no history of psychoneurosis previous to their combat experience. Exceptionally acute cases were transferred to the 96th General Hospital. The Red Cross worked alongside the medical personnel to cater for the N.P. patients. Some of the Red Cross members attended weekly lectures on psychiatry given by the two neuropsychiatric officers to the other offices of the Medical Service. From November 1944 the Red Cross set aside periods during the week for teaching craftwork to the N.P. patients and a small craft shop was installed in the N.P. ward.

The Assistant Field Director describes the setting up of the shop:

"The men worked like Trojans to make a practical and convenient shop. Except for a general lack of certain tools the place is well equipped and is open most of the day for patients of the ward" (53rd A.R.C. Archives).

In January 1945 two of the N.P. wards made an afghan out of a number of coloured woven squares of rug wool. One of the nurses on the wards sewed together the squares once the men had made them and then sent it on a tour of the wards to show other bed patients.

The Red Cross also involved the N.P. patients in a show they developed called: 'We're Buzzing.' It featured Hill Billy music, jitterbug, tap dancing and skits. The AFD commented on it:

" ... these patients appear to derive much benefit from their participation in the show and from having to handle the little responsibilities that seem to go with such a project" (53rd A.R.C. Archives).

A rehabilitation programme at the 53rd had been instituted shortly after the hospital opened. The programme was organised primarily to:

" ... recondition patients for their return to duty following their hospitalisation" (53rd General Hospital Archives).

This was mainly aimed at the non Z.I. patients although all patients took part in the rehabilitation programme even the non-ambulatory patients.

Physical Therapy Department.
(J. Brinkman).

As part of their rehabilitation programme patients were enlisted to help with odd jobs like handling the large volume of mail that came in daily and in operating the patients mess. They were also enlisted to help with the loading and unloading of patients from hospital trains.

The ambulatory rehabilitation group were known as trainees as their rehabilitation work was designed to train them to be fit for duty. The trainees occupied four wards and three tents on the medical ramp with a capacity of 192 beds. Officer trainees occupied private rooms, a capacity of 24 beds. A medical officer checked the trainees once a week and placed them in the correct class for their condition. The senior officer trainee acted as Commanding Officer of the Training Company and the other officer trainees acted as his assistants.

In October 1944 the Rehabilitation section moved into the buildings formerly put aside for the Venereal Disease section. A gymnasium built entirely by trainees out of scrap lumber was completed in December. The equipment consisted of horizontal and parallel bars, weights and pulling machines, a basketball net, two pounding bags, wrestling mats and medicine balls.

Also in December arrangements were made for the rapid transfer of trainees with less than 75 days hospitalisation to Rehabilitation and Reconditioning Centres, thus freeing the 53rd to concentrate more on accommodating and evacuating the Z.I. patients. The strength of the trainee detachment dropped from 200 to 75 and the remainder of the trainees were moved into tents.

Rehabilitation and Reconditioning Centres had been set up towards the end of 1944 to free more beds in the general hospitals. In Bromsgrove,

Rehabilitation patients at 123rd Station Hospital, Bromsgrove
(123rd Station Hospital Archives).

Worcestershire the 77th Station Hospital and 123rd Reconditioning hospital
took enlisted men and officers respectively. The 307th Rehabilitation Centre,
based in Stoneleigh, Warwickshire took non-neuropsychiatric ambulatory
patients who did not require special diets and could be rehabilitated in the
E.T.O.

Chapter 11

RECREATION AND WELFARE

The work of the Red Cross unit at Merebrook fell into two categories, recreation and welfare. The Recreation workers worked closely with the Special Service Section of the 53rd.

At Oulton Park Colonel Brandstadt met with the Red Cross girls and set out his plans for them to assist a committee of officers and nurses in planning recreation for the men of the detachment. At the meeting the Colonel indicated that he intended for the Red Cross to plan its activities with as much freedom as possible, consulting the other military personnel within the unit on matters of detail.

The first Red Cross project at Oulton Park was planned in conjunction with the Special Service, Transportation Section, P.X. Section and Mess Section. The girls planned a party for the men of the detachment, off base. Fortunately one of the detachment men knew a local lady, Mrs Weedal, who helped the girls to locate a suitable venue. When the girls decided on a large parish school she helped them to apply for the permits needed so that the party could end later than 11p.m.

The Special Service Officer arranged for the band of an engineer's unit that was also based on the post to play at the party and the P.X. Officer put aside 540 bottles of Coca Cola. The Transportation Officer provided the transport. Jane Whitacre, the Senior Recreation worker, described the 'advance party' for the dance in her report:

"At five thirty in the evening of the party a large truck rolled past the main gate of the post bearing our Red Cross staff and a volunteer K.P. detail of four sergeants and a corporal deployed at random among large bags of bread, boxes of cookies, the precious colas, containers of sandwich spreads, various kitchen utensils all in addition to the P.A. system lent for the occasion" (53rd A.R.C. Archives).

Girls from the local community had been invited as guests and they arrived shortly after the detachment men. The Red Cross had planned to play some 'icebreaking games' to get the party going but the band leader, who had played for similar parties before, suggested that the band play some English numbers like the Lambeth Walk, Boomps a Daisy and the Hokey Cokey to start with.

A.R.C. unit. Standing L-R May Esther Weikel (Secretary), Clara Neustadt, (Senior Recreation Worker), Alma Klinger (Staff aide). Front row: L-R Elaine Wakefield (Assistant Field Director), Jane Porter (Recreation Worker) (53rd General Hospital Year Book).

"Accordingly we ran off a grand march with one of our own sergeants as MC and followed this up immediately with the series of dances mentioned by the band leader, who proved to be exactly correct. The girls taught the boys their dances and the G.I.s reciprocated with some 'yank jiving'. From then on the dance floor literally shook and the party was on assured success ... At midnight the 'Star Spangled Banner' and 'God Save the King' signalled the finale and the party broke up. The clean up squad cleared the debris and the kitchen equipment and we returned to camp in a G.I. ambulance" (53rd A.R.C. Archives).

Following this the Red Cross were invited to make and preside over the refreshments for the opening dance of the Officer and Nurses club on the post and at the three other dances that followed they made decorations and generally offered assistance where needed.

When the 53rd moved to Merebrook Camp the girls intended to plan similar parties but they found it was necessary to organise dances on a cooperative basis with the other hospitals in the area as there was only one

The Winter Gardens (M. Collins).

dance hall (the Winter Gardens) available and this had already been booked in advance for two Thursdays each month for the use of the 19th General Hospital based at Blackmore Park. However the girls did help to plan for a ball in Malvern to mark the last day of Salute the Soldier Week.

The unit also contributed to planning the opening dance for the Doughnut Dugout in Malvern which took place on 29th September 1944. The Recreation Workers and Staff Aide from the 53rd were assisted by a committee of two Detachment men and Corporal Segura who painted murals in the room which had been assigned to the 53rd. The room received first prize in the inter-hospital contest for decorating rooms. The dance was attended by groups of patients from all of the nearby hospitals.

Once established at Merebrook the girls started investigating the possibilities of arranging tours for the personnel. On March 17th they organised a bicycle tour, the following week a combination of bus trip and walk and the next week a trip to Cheltenham and Tewkesbury.

On 23rd April, the day before the first patients arrived, a 'Yankee Picnic' was organised for the detachment. Colonel Johnstone, the Head of Civil Defence in the area owned a farm and he offered the girls the use of one of his fields. The girls contacted officers of the local WRENs, WAFs and ATS units to invite about 100 girls. The men were also permitted to bring their own dates so about 300 girls were present. Mary Cox Bryan, the Assistant Field Director, describes the end of the picnic:

"The climax of the afternoon came at 'chowtime' when everyone gathered around the bonfires and roasted their weenies on pointed sticks. Our Mess hall personnel really did the 53rd proud and served a feast of potato salad, homemade hot dog rolls, weenies, coffee and chocolate cake. Our Motor Pool provided transportation to and from the town for the girls and also for the food and mess equipment from the post. The party seemed to be universally enjoyed by the girls, G.I.s and several local civilians of all ages who gathered round to watch the fun" (53rd A.R.C. Archives).

When the hospital opened for patients the Red Cross realised that the nature of the Recreational Programme would need to change to centre mainly on the patients instead of the detachment personnel. It was necessary to cancel the trip to Stratford upon Avon that had been planned for the detachment personnel in May.

On the arrival of the patients it was also necessary to adapt the Red Cross working hours. The girls were requested not to conduct recreational activities on the wards until 2.15p.m. and not until 4.30p.m. for ambulatory patients because of the rehabilitation programmes. In the mornings all patients were expected to be either on their ward or at rehabilitation classes. However the Red Cross soon found that the patients expected to be able to use the Red Cross facilities at all hours when they were not otherwise occupied. When the girls informed Colonel Brandstadt he gave them permission to commence activities at 1.30p.m.

Doughnut dugout in Malvern (53rd General Hospital Archives).

Left: Arnold Wallace and colleagues in a park nearby the hospital (A. Wallace).
Right: Men of the Detachment on home made bicycle (J. Brinkman).

The girls hoped that the Patients Rehabilitation Programme would help them by providing patients to carry out some of the work that needed doing in their buildings like building a fireplace and shelving in the Recreation Hall. Unfortunately the Rehabilitation Officer would not sanction this although he did expect the girls to provide a craft project scheduled as part of the rehabilitation programme. The girls attempted to explain that this was not Red Cross policy but the officer continued to send patients to the Red Cross for supplies and assigned them the craftwork they had begun with the Red Cross to complete within their Rehabilitation timetable. After several futile attempts to reason with the officer the girls approached Colonel Brandstadt who reinforced their position. Shortly after this the Rehabilitation Officer was replaced.

On their arrival at Merebrook the girls had decided to split up and share the nurses living quarters rather than be billeted in one hut altogether. They were given the use of the patient's recreation room for their activities. This was a large room with a stage at one end. A screen for watching movies was erected permanently above the stage. Corporal Segura had painted a mural background for the stage and dressing rooms complete with dressing tables, mirrors and lights were constructed off stage. The girls arranged for cabinets with moveable shelves to be built at the opposite end of the room. These could be moved to make an enclosed space for crafts. The girls also requested that a pitch mastic floor be built on top of the existing concrete floor and after several conferences with the Commanding Officer and the British contractors the floor was put down and paid for out of hospital funds.

The Recreation Hall was officially opened on 1st May with a 'Welcome to our City Party' for the patients. Mary Cox Bryan describes the party in her report:

"As each guest came in the hall he was handed 'the key to the city' – a paper tally in the shape of a key. There were approximately 100 guests at the party and they were divided by the tallies into five groups. Each group played a different game and progressed to the next one after a specified length of time. A unified scoring system was worked out for each game. A variety of games were played, demanding of necessity, a minimum of equipment" (53rd A.R.C. Archives).

The games included darts, tossing potatoes into a box, scrambled G.I. words, sculpturing objects from chewing gum, wire, string and other materials to hand and cutting out pictures from magazines of what the patients would most like to have and displaying them on a clothes line. In the latter game there was a large display of pin up girls. At the end of the evening the scores were combined and prizes given to the highest totals. Members of the detachment produced a stage show while refreshments of fresh lemonade and cookies were served.

The girls scheduled parties in the Recreation Hall once a week. A number of different groups of girls were invited to the parties, the most popular group being the WRENs from the nearby training station. Colonel Brandstadt did not allow dancing at the patients' parties (except rehabilitation patients) so the parties usually consisted of progressive games and refreshments. The girls noticed that the crutch, cane and cast group were more or less forced into the background to escape being crushed by the more agile patients at the parties so they organised one party specifically for those with crutches, canes or casts.

The Special Service Section was instrumental in putting together a dance band for the 53rd. Instruments were ordered and auditions held. Seven musicians were chosen to comprise the dance band which played for the detachment rehabilitation and officer dances on the post as well as for private dances off the post.

The Red Cross also arranged for entertainment groups to visit the hospital to perform in the Recreation Hall. The group 'Sweet and Swing' presented five ward shows to the patients in the afternoon and one evening to the ambulatory patients in the Recreation Hall. Mary Cox Bryon noted that although the patients enjoyed the show:

Red Cross Clubmobile which visited the 53rd regularly (J. Brinkman).

" ... *it is hoped that in the future the material for the shows will be more carefully selected ... We don't feel that there is any place in a Red Cross show for smutty and ... corny so called humour. It was painfully embarrassing for the Red Cross staff to sit aside and listen whenever the Mistress of Ceremonies came on stage"* (53rd ARC).

More edifying for the men were the visits of the Local Baptist Church Choir. Rosemary Williams' parents were members of the choir and used to sing to the soldiers in the hospitals local to Malvern. She remembers her parents telling her that the badly wounded patients at Merebrook especially appreciated the singing. Other visitors to the hospital included Joe Louis the world Heavyweight Champion, who visited on June 28th 1944. Bob Garrison remembers shaking hands with him. Jack Dempsey, the ex-champion also made an unannounced informal visit later in the year.

In January 1945 the hospital played host to Sir Alexander Fleming. Professor Fleming told the 150 medical officers at the hospital about his work in the laboratories of St. Marys Hospital in London that led to his discovery of the mould, 'Penicillin Notatatum.' At this time Penicillin was the only antibiotic available to the armed forces and it had saved countless lives. Reporting on the visit the Malvern Gazette wrote:

"This discovery, which will undoubtedly be reckoned as one of the major advances in the treatment of disease will, In the post war world, be available to all who need it" (Malvern Gazette 13/1/45).

Ruby Johnson remembers meeting the Professor who commented that the hospital was so clean that he would never have discovered penicillin there.

Another distinguished visitor to the hospital was HRH the Princess Royal. The hospital was also visited by a number of inspecting parties. General Hawley, the E.T.O. Chief Surgeon, visited the hospital twice. On 13th July he was accompanied by General Norman T Kirk, the Army Surgeon General, as well as several other officers. They made a thorough inspection of the wards, paying particular attention to the treatment of fractures from the battle front.

On 17th August Congresswoman Bolton of Ohio visited several wards of the hospital extending greetings to many of the wounded soldiers, particularly those from her home state.

The Red Cross were not the only group to have the use of the Recreation Hall. The Special Service used it to show movies three times a week. Each time there were two performances, the first for the patients and the second for the detachment and officer personnel (The Special Service also showed movies on about ten wards each week). The Rehabilitation Group also used the hall for

Sir Alexander Fleming with the Commanding Officer of the Hospital.

SIR ALEXANDER FLEMING, the discoverer of Penicillin, was the guest of the Medical Hospital Centre at a meeting held at a U.S. Army General Hospital, in Worcestershire, on Sunday. He was introduced to a group of 150 medical officers by the Commanding Officer of that hospital.

Professor Fleming told the audience about his work in the laboratories of St. Mary's Hospital, London, that led to his discovery of the germ arresting properties of the mould called *Penicillium Notatum*. This mould produces a substance that is thousands of times more destructive to disease germs than carbolic acid. This substance now called Penicillin acts without injuring the human body. At present the available supply of penicillin is largely confined to use in the armed forces where it has proved its efficiency by saving countless lives.

This discovery which will undoubtedly be reckoned as one of the major advances in the treatment of disease will in the postwar world be available to all who need it. The experience in its use gained by medical officers in the Service will be a powerful aid in combating hitherto fatal diseases.

After a midday meal at the Officers' Mess, Sir Alexander visited the laboratories of the hospital. The modern and com-

MALVERN THEATRE

Phone MALVERN 777.

TO-DAY: 2306 WOMEN Phyllis Calvert
SUNDAY: Cont. from 3.45. Doors 3.15
Brian Donlevy in NIGHTMARE

ALL NEXT WEEK
SPECIAL TIMES AND PRICES
Twice Daily 1.15, 5.45. NOT Cont.
Doors Open 12.45, 5.15
Prices 1/6, 2/9, 3/6
Seats CANNOT be Booked!

Great Jewel of Motion Picture Art
Margaret Mitchell's story of the Old South in Technicolor

Gone With The Wind

Top left: Princess Royal at the 53rd (53rd General Hospital Archives).
Top right: Malvern Gazette 13.01.1945. Bottom left: Alexander Fleming with
Colonel Brandstadt at the 53rd. (53rd General Hospital Archives).
Bottom right: Royal visit (53rd General Hospital Year Book).

their programme. This meant that there was a constant stream of personnel through the hall and the Red Cross supplies began to go missing.

The Red Cross found it difficult to cover their entire programme in the Recreation Hall because of its other uses so they put in a request for more space. They were given rooms in a ward which they used as offices, storage and a temporary craft shop.

Unfortunately on 26th May orders came through for all wards to be vacated and set up in readiness for a large influx of patients. The Recreation Department moved to one end of the tailor shop and a tent and supplies were stored in the kitchen of the officers and nurses club.

Officers' Club (53rd General Hospital Year Book).

A Detachment Day room was set up in a wing of what had been the British Welfare Canteen for the use of construction workers. It was equipped with chairs, writing tables, books, radio, record player, table tennis, snooker and a small table games. Corporal Segura decorated the walls with a series of murals. A small bar was built at one end and beer was sold there six nights a week.

On June 19th the Red Cross moved into the other wing of the canteen which became their permanent quarters. The building was still incomplete at this point but the girls thought that if they moved in it might help to speed the work up. Mary Cox Bryon regarded it as an inferior building with:

"Tar paper walls, unfinished cement floors and leaking roof" (A.R.C.)

In July the supply depot at Malvern link made curtains for the building to brighten up the room and the girls pinned up patients art work on the walls. One patient made a brightly coloured poster for the craft work which read:

"Thinkin' of making somethin'?" and offered suggestions for crafts. The girls found the poster seemed to attract patients to the craft shop. It took until September 1944 for the girls to get the outside of the building and the cement floors painted. An enlisted man was assigned to the building to serve as an odd job man.

At the beginning of 1945 a Nissen hut was constructed for the use of the Red Cross as a workshop for patients. It was operated and supervised full time by detachment men. Elaine Wakefield describes the workshop:

"At any one time one can find the hut filled with busy hands at hammers, saws, files, chisels and soldering irons. We have been amazed at the attractive items which the patients have made in the shop" (53rd A.R.C. Archives).

One of the local residents sold the girls a small hand loom to use and a weaving project was set up. The patients also enjoyed leather craft and making items from plexiglass. Unfortunately difficulties in obtaining supplies held up some of the craft work. The girls were able to contact Mr Gimson, Managing Director of the Royal Worcester Porcelain Company. He agreed to furnish slip and moulds for the making of ash trays, dishes and small figures and also to fire the articles once the patients had cast them.

From October 1944 instruction classes in crafts were held in the Red Cross building twice weekly for ambulatory patients to learn new skills and to get ideas to help non-ambulatory patients on the wards with craft work. Elaine Wakefield writes:

" ... the ambulatory patients were a great help in getting instructions and materials at Red Cross and relaying them back to bed patients" (53rd A.R.C. Archives).

It was difficult for the craft worker to get around all the wards so this use of ambulatory patients meant that bed patients got the opportunity to partake in the craft programme.

Until September 1944 the girls had been unable to take up offers from the WVS and similar local organisations which had offered hospitality to the patients. Mary Cox Bryon wrote in her report:

"These people are constantly calling up with offers of outings or visits to homes in the locality and parties for our patients. This type of thing we now find is contrary to the policy of the hospital and we have been obliged to decline a number of invitations offered to our patients" (53rd A.R.C. Archives).

In September the hospital authorities agreed to provide transport for patient outings. Three trips were arranged for this month. A group of 100 patients attended an afternoon tea given by the Mayor and Civic Reception Committee at Malvern. 25 attended a tea at the Guild Hall in Worcester and twelve had Sunday afternoon tea in a private home in Malvern. Patients in the Rehabilitation Programme were given bi-weekly excursions with transport.

In November a public address system was installed throughout the hospital by the Red Cross with outlets in all the wards. A contest was conducted throughout the hospital for an appropriate name. The name selected was 4UGI and a formal ceremony dedicating the broadcasting station was arranged. Not only was the system a source of entertainment it was also used to reach the wards with announcements of various kinds. A radio staff was appointed with patients acting as directors, talent scouts and broadcasters. A popular daily programme was the Record Request Hour. Lists of the records in the ARC music library were posted in the wards and patients submitted their requests and dedications which were played the following day.

Early in November the Red Cross started making plans for the Christmas activities at the hospital. The girls arranged for forty orphan boys aged four to twelve from the Good Shepherd home to put on a nativity play for the patients and also arranged for each ward to 'adopt' one of the boys for the day. In the run up to Christmas a number of patients made presents for their 'adopted child'.

On Christmas day the boys were invited to eat Christmas dinner on the ward and then they were given candy, pennies and toys by the patients. The Red Cross noticed that the patients enjoyed themselves as much as the boys. The boys remained on the ward all afternoon and then put on their nativity play in the Recreation Hall. The event was reported in the Malvern Gazette.

On Christmas evening the Red Cross held a party for the patients with party games on a Christmas theme being played. The Red Cross also held a New Year's party which featured a musical baseball contest and a horse race where patients participated as contestants and betters. Tickets were distributed to take the place of money for the placing of the bets which were later 'cashed in' for prizes.

Alongside the recreation work the Red Cross had a social work case load. The girls attempted to deal with a variety of problems amongst the patients, many of them related to families back home or their injuries. A number of patients wanted to contact their family who were in England or Europe.

One patient who wanted to contact his twin brother was about to be discharged and sent back to duty. The man wanted to be assigned to his brother's unit. The Red Cross were able to arrange for the soldier to travel to a Red Cross Club near the camp where his twin brother was located but unfortunately by the time the man got there his twin's unit had moved on.

However the personnel of the Red Cross Club were able to assist him in finding the new location and make reservations at the Red Cross Club in the locality. Eventually the patient was able to meet up with his brother and initiate proceedings regarding his transfer.

Families of patients would often write to the Red Cross to find out about their loved ones. Up to July 1944 the unit were prevented from replying to the enquiries by Colonel Brandstadt because of Censorship Circular number 47 which prohibited writing about battle casualties. When the girls requested clarification from Headquarters they were informed that this rule did not apply to official Red Cross communication. However the Colonel was not easily persuaded and would not allow the girls to send welfare reports until he had had clarification from the office of the Chief Surgeon.

In September 1944 the girls received five requests for health and welfare reports of the men of the detachment. In three of the cases the families'

Christmas menu from the 53rd General Hospital c.1944.
(Brian Iles Malvern Museum Collection).

Top left: Malvern Gazette December 1944. Top right and bottom right: Christmas 1944 (J. Brinkman). Bottom left: Letter sent from the 53rd General Hospital just prior to Christmas 1944. (Authors' collection).

concerns were caused by erroneous notices in the home newspaper that the men had been wounded in action. The three men were all members of the hospital detachment and had never been in combat.

The Red Cross were also able to provide some support for the small number of French patients in the hospital. During October and November 1944 some of the French patients met with the other patients three times a week to study each other's languages although:

"How instructive these periods were cannot be ascertained but they certainly appeared to afford great amusement to all concerned" (53rd A.R.C. Archives).

Contacts were made with local groups interested in the Free French Forces and through these groups a number of French books and records were obtained. Local residents visited the hospital to chat with the French patients in their own language. On one occasion the Red Cross presided over a small tea party for the French patients and the owner of a local farm who brought with her an invalided French Officer who was her house guest.

Chapter 12

A BIGGER JOB THAN WAS EXPECTED

V.E. day passed quietly at the hospital at Merebrook. It was necessary for the medical and surgical departments to treat it as any other day as the patients still needed to be cared for.

Bob Garrison from the Pharmacy Department was on leave in London on May 8th 1945. He had put in for a three day pass some weeks before, not having any idea of the significance of the date. He remembers waking up on the Monday and seeing crowds of people in the streets, celebrating. He walked down Regent Street, where girls ran up to him and kissed him. Later he walked over to Buckingham Palace and climbed up on the Victoria Monument in front of the palace to see the Royal family and later, Winston Churchill.

Ruby Johnson was also on leave in London when V.E. day was declared. She remembers the crowds of people celebrating in Piccadilly Circus and buses stranded there unable to move because of the crowds.

After V.E. Day there was a reduction in the amount of casualties received at the hospital. The 120 day rule which meant that patients were kept at the hospital if they could be returned to duty within 120 days in the U.K. was reduced to 60 days. This meant many more patients were eligible to return home.

By 17th August all the patients had been sent home and the 53rd was informed that it would be taking over the nearby neuropsychiatric hospital at Brickbarns, Plant 4174, the site occupied by the 312th Station Hospital and formerly by the 96th General Hospital. The hospital site at Merebrook was completely closed and equipment and supplies superfluous to requirement at the new site were returned to the appropriate depots. The site was handed over to the British authorities on 31st August 1945.

On 1st August vehicles from nearby hospital units that had already been closed down were assigned to the 53rd and these vehicles were useful for transporting equipment and personnel to Brickbarns. The motor pool was able to handle the entire move.

The civilian personnel from Merebrook were also transferred to Brickbarns to join the civilian personnel already working on the site, giving a total of 83

Bob Garrison, on leave in London (R. Garrison).

employees. After making a survey of the number of civilian personnel needed 43 were discharged.

Meanwhile Colonel Brandstadt had been transferred to the 192nd General Hospital on July 5th and was replaced by Lieutenant Colonel Gordon C. McRae who was formerly the Commanding Officer of the 347th Station Hospital. On 12th September Colonel McRae left to take command of the 182nd General Hospital and Colonel George H. Daniel, the former Commanding Officer of the 801st Hospital Center, took command.

When the 53rd arrived at Brickbarns the 6th Medical Depot and the 266th Finance Disbursing section were staging there but they were transferred to the Port of Embarkation shortly after the arrival of the 53rd.

When the 53rd moved to Brickbarns the 101 neuropsychiatric patients were transferred from the 312th Station Hospital to the 53rd. These men had not yet been returned to the U.S. as they had been labelled 'irreclaimable.'

Officers' Club at Brickbarns (J. Brinkman).

The personnel of the 53rd made every effort to treat these patients effectively although they had had very little experience in treating neuropsychiatric patients. Previously, while based at Merebrook the 53rd had transferred their psychotic patients to the 96th General Hospital at Brickbarns.

Alongside the N.P. patients Brickbarns had a number of Z.I. patients. As other hospitals in the vicinity had closed down and left, remaining patients were sent to Brickbarns. Three critically ill patients, who were admitted as a nearby hospital evacuated its patients, all had a fatal termination, two within a week of their admittance.

Enlisted Men's Area at Brickbarns (J. Brinkman).

The hospital also acted as a station hospital for troops based in the vicinity. The Surgical Section was kept active during their time at Brickbarns as, although there were a decreasing number of battle casualties being admitted, there was an increasing number of non-battle injuries and operative diseases incurred by the troops stationed in the area now served by the hospital.

A number of the N.P. patients at the hospital were registered as 'prisoners'. The majority of these were being held for examination to determine sanity. Taking care of and guarding prisoners called for additional manpower and it was necessary to train some of the detachment personnel as guards. The archivist for the 53rd records:

"The ward men learnt rapidly and little trouble was experienced in their care" *(53rd General Hospital Archives).*

The 53rd were functioning with reduced manpower at Brickbarns as after V.E. Day a number of the personnel were assigned to other hospitals that would be redeployed to the Pacific where the fighting continued. Bob Garrison was sent back to the U.S. for a thirty day furlough before being deployed to the Pacific. He left Greenock, Scotland at the beginning of August 1945 on the Queen Elizabeth. While he was on board the news came through of the dropping of the atom bombs on Hiroshima and Nagasaki. Bob recalls reading the news on the ship's newspaper and still remembers the feeling of relief at the thought that the war in the Pacific was over and he would be able to return home.

Nurse Ruby Johnson also sailed home on the Queen Elizabeth for a furlough before her intended redeployment to the Pacific. She remembers that the ship was very crowded because of the large number of personnel travelling home. She remembers seeing Princess Wilhelmina of the Netherlands and her lady in waiting strolling on the deck. The staterooms originally intended for two billeted eight female personnel. This time the voyage took only five days as there was no need for the zig zag course. Due to the cold climate when they left England the nurses were dressed in wool uniforms and Ruby remembers feeling very uncomfortable when the ship docked in New York where the weather was hot and humid. As New York Harbor came into sight Ruby recalls:

"The statue of Liberty in New York Harbor was a sight I will never forget. I knew I was home."

Back at Brickbarns the shortage of personnel caused problems across the hospital. The motor pool in particular struggled to maintain its large selection of vehicles with the small number of staff. There was no Rehabilitation Section in operation at this time which meant that there were no convalescing patients available to assist in policing the area and tidying up the grounds which were in a poor state when the 53rd arrived. New personnel were assigned to the hospital but many of these were untrained and needed supervision and orientation in their duties.

Some hospitals had been using German Prisoner of War labour in the latter part of the war and a stockade had been built on the site of the 93rd General Hospital at Blackmore Park for this purpose but because of the top secret radar laboratory located in Malvern German prisoners could not be used in the area and so 35 British soldiers were billeted at Brickbarns temporarily while they took down the stockade.

Journey home on the Queen Mary (J. Brinkman).

There was an almost complete turnover of nurses during this period. Married nurses were sent home with the exception of a few key specialists, the majority of which were surgical nurses. New nurses were assigned to the 53rd but:

"The morale of the new nurses coming into the unit was low as they had been separated from their units, most of which were returning to the States and the nurses felt an injustice had been done to them" (53rd General Hospital Archives).

There were some advantages for the nurses stationed at Brickbarns. As so many nurses had been sent home the remaining female personnel had the luxury of living only two or three to a hut. Each nurse was also granted a 72 hour pass each month and nearly all the nurses were given seven days temporary duty at the Nurses Rest Home at Felixstowe.

A nurse and officer from the 53rd were married during the post V.E. Day period. The couple were married on 25 July at St. Mary's Catholic Church in Hanley Swan. A reception was held at the Officers' club where the Mess personnel of the 53rd provided a wedding cake. After the reception the couple had pride of place at the noon day meal in the Officer's Mess where the 53rd's dance band played the music.

This was not the only romance within the unit. Previously Nurse, 1st Lieutenant Catherine Murphy had married Sergeant Elenzer Carrol Bagley at the same church. The bride had been given away by Colonel Brandstadt. There was a large group of hospital staff at the wedding and reception which followed at the Officers' club. This wedding was unusual as it was against military regulations for an officer to date an enlisted man.

Another nurse who dated an enlisted man was Ruby Johnson. While at Merebrook Ruby often went bicycle riding in the countryside with Melville Williams, a lab technician. Regulations stated that Class A uniforms must be worn off base so Ruby remembers that she had to ride in a skirt. Sometimes the couple would meet up in the lobby of a hotel. Ruby remembers that if the news came on the radio they would have to talk quietly as the British liked to listen intently to all the war news. The pair would often attend the theatre but would ensure

TWO ALL-AMERICAN WEDDINGS

Solemnised at Local Hospitals

Two all-American weddings were solemnised in Malvern last week-end.

Capt. Thelda Derr, chief nurse of the 93rd General Hospital (aided by Miss Duffey and the Red Cross staff) gave a reception for Second-Lieut. Shirley Craig and First-Lieut. Paul Carlson at the Red Cross centre at the hospital. This followed the ceremony at the hospital chapel, conducted by Chaplain W. H. Rittenhouse, when the bride—who wore a lovely white satin gown—was given away by the C.O., Col. U. R. Merigangas.

The song "Because" was beautifully sung during the ceremony by Lieut (Nurse) Faber. Both the service and the reception were largely attended, the bride being a popular member of the nursing staff and the bridegroom a former patient.

Last Thursday week the Catholic Church at Hanley Swan was the scene of another wedding in which both bride and groom were Ameri-

1st Lt. Murphy and M/Sgt. Bagley

can. They were First-Lieut. Catherine Murphy and Master/Sergt. Elenzer Carroll Bagley, and both were in service uniform.

The bride was given away by the C.O. of the 53rd General Hospital, Col. Wayne Brandstadt, and the service was conducted by Fr. H. Richardson and Chaplain Hunt. There was a large crowd of U.S. hospital staff and patients at the service, and at the reception which followed at the officers' club.

Malvern Gazette.

Chapter 13

231ST STATION HOSPITAL

The 231st Station Hospital had been awaiting transport to be redeployed in the Pacific when V.J. Day was announced. The orders were then rescinded and the unit was sent to Fairford in Gloucestershire.

Detachment A of the 231st was assigned to Brickbarns to run the hospital which was now functioning as the only neuropsychiatric unit in the U.K. Of the 325 patients left in the hospital at this point 50 were closed ward patients and approximately 100 were open ward neuropsychiatric cases. The remainder of the patient population consisted of various medical and surgical cases. One of the patients, Rex Blevins, from Washington State, was actually a civilian who had been employed by the British Ministry of Fuel and Power. As well as the patients in the hospital the 231st was responsible for a large out patient population from the units in the surrounding area.

The Commanding Officer of the 231st was Lieutenant Colonel S.E. King and he held responsibility for both the main group at Fairford and Detachment A at Brickbarns. Lieutenant Colonel King, from New York, was a former Assistant Professor of Medicine at Columbia University and had been a practising doctor for 20 years. In the Malvern Gazette he was quoted as saying that:

" … he and his compatriots will carry back to the States many happy memories of English goodwill and hospitality" (Malvern Gazette 20.10.1945).

Unfortunately his memories of England probably had a bitter taste as on November 10 Lieutenant Colonel King was relieved of his command and demoted pending possible court martial because of his inefficiency and mishandling of his responsibilities.

Prior to this date there had been a number of complaints about Colonel King, particularly from the Assistant Field Director for the Red Cross unit at Fairford. Leato Martin complained that on 29 October 1945 Colonel King had announced that the Red Cross facilities were off limits to all personnel of the two staging hospitals located on the post at Fairford. As the Assistant Field Director of the Red Cross Leato stated that in her opinion the Red Cross facilities could accommodate any personnel who wished to use them.

Leato went on to explain that Colonel King disliked having the units staging on the post as he resented the additional responsibility. Colonel King also refused to allow the units the use of any Special Service facilities. As soon as the Colonel made these announcements there was protest from the personnel of the staging units. In an official report Miss Martin stated that all the members of the hospital post:

" *... resented his presence, find him domineering, demanding and restricting" (231st A.R.C. Archives).*

She also reported that officers and Red Cross personnel were required to report to his office if they wished to go off base even in off duty time. He wanted to know where they were going, what they proposed to do and how long they would be.

Leato Martin also complained that Colonel King was 'offensively attentive' to her both in the office and around the post. Amongst other things he had ordered her to go away with him and when she had refused he stated that it was an order and she could not refuse. As a result of the complaints Colonel King was removed from his position and on 10 November 1945 Major Winning took over the command of the two posts.

Three Red Cross members were assigned to Brickbarns with the 231st. They were led by Rose Daniels who had formerly served with the 93rd General Hospital at Blackmore Park. The Red Cross units attached to the 96th General, 312th Station and 53rd General Hospitals had left most of their equipment and supplies on site so the unit was not short of equipment. As there were only three Red Cross Staff it was difficult to implement a full Red Cross Programme so the girls made arrangements for a trained volunteer to come in to do craft work with the men for four half days per week. This meant that the Staff Aide could be released for ward work.

NEW U.S. HOSPITAL UNIT

Takes Up Quarters At The Wells

Malvern, which a few weeks ago said an official farewell to U.S. medical corps' personnel who had been occupying five hospital sites in the district during the war, is now welcoming a new hospital unit, the 231st Station Hospital, which moved in about a month ago to the former 96th U.S. Hospital at the Wells.

The commanding officer, Lieut.-Col. S. E. King, who is also in command of a hospital unit at Fairford, Cirencester, said he had found Malvern people very friendly, and that they were returning hospitality extended to the patients and personnel by arranging regular Saturday evening dances.

Col. King, who is a former Assistant Professor of Medicine at Columbia University, and a practising doctor for 20 years, comes from New York State. He is a keen advocate of Anglo-American relations, and says that he and his compatriots will carry back to the States many happy memories of English goodwill and hospitality.

General medical and surgical cases are undertaken by this unit, and the patients come mainly from Cardiff docks and Ashchurch, though, of course, numbers of them come from other parts of the country, often in the station's own stretcher car conveyance.

One of the patients at the present time is an American civilian, Mr. Rex Blevins, from Washington State, who has been working for the British Ministry of Fuel and Power.

The unit was formerly stationed near Cirencester and south of Norwich. It has about 200-300 patients, and a small but efficient staff of surgeons and nurses. Capt. C. Kellgren is adjutant, a busy and important post, and he it is who makes many of the arrangements for the social events.

RED CROSS CLUB

Capt. Achilles C. Lisle is executive officer, and one of the chief surgeons. He hails from Oklahoma, and has been in this country 16 months, but three of these were spent in France. He was once for a short period with the old 55th General Hospital in Malvern whose C.O. at that time was Col. Gill. Major Winning, from the Fairford unit, is surgeon-in-chief, and visits the hospital at frequent intervals. He comes from Brooklyn and has many good-humoured arguments with the colonel about the respective merits of that place, and of New York State.

There is an active Red Cross club centre (always the hub of a U.S. hospital) of which Miss R. Daniels, of New York, is in charge. Miss Daniels is also not a stranger to the district, for she succeeded Miss Duffey as Red Cross director of the 93rd Hospital, once located at Blackmore Park.

Miss Daniels proudly shows visitors the comfortable lounge in which patients can read (there is a well-equipped library) play games (there is a special room for)

Malvern Gazette.

The girls also enlisted volunteers from the community to assist with the Recreation Programme.

The Assistant Field Director, Rose Daniels, was much in demand for social work during the time that the 231st were at Brickbarns. This was mainly due to the large percentage of neuropsychiatric patients and those with acute syphilitic and gonorrhoeal infections. Long periods of waiting for transportation home with frequent passes for the Z.I. patients meant that loans were frequently requested from the Red Cross.

Because many patients were just filling in time until they returned home the girls were able to organise trips to places like Stratford upon Avon and the Malvern Hills. They also organised parties in the Recreation Hall. In October there was a birthday party for all patients with a birthday in October and at the end of the month there was a Halloween party. The closed ward patients made the decorations and one closed ward patient, who was an accomplished pianist, was allowed to come and play for the guests. The girls used candlelight to create the right atmosphere. The patients served one another and the guests, popped corn and presided over the drinks. There was a costume competition with one patient from each ward dressing up.

Although the girls were busy the Red Cross unit did not come off well in an inspection by Catherine C. Hiatt, the Administrative Assistant supervising the Red Cross. On 29 September Miss Hiatt inspected the unit and found:

" ... a surprising lack of focus" (231st A.R.C. Archives).

In the Red Cross activities on the post. She made several scathing remarks about Rose Daniels' attitude, stating that she found her 'dogmatic'. During the interview with Rose Daniels, Miss Hiatt shut the door to which Rose remonstrated that:

" ... this door is never closed, they don't understand it" (231st A.R.C. Archives).

Miss Hiatt complained to Rose that the Red Cross building was open too many hours, not giving the detachment men time to clean the building while it was empty, but Rose's reply to this was:

"This is the patient's building and they have got a right to have it available to them" (231st A.R.C. Archives).

Miss Hiatt's final comment was:

"The Assistant Field Director appears to have certain perceived ideas regarding her operation, she seems uninterested in supervisory support and finds difficulty in accepting suggestions given" (231st A.R.C. Archives).

During September and October the patient population at the hospital slowly decreased and in November the hospital was reclassified. The neuropsychiatric division of the hospital was closed and the patients sent back to the U.S. The Commanding Officer requested that one of the Red Cross workers who were familiar with the closed ward patients accompany the hospital train to Southampton. The Red Cross worker put together a carefully planned programme for the entire period of travel so that the men would be occupied and more relaxed. Fortunately the trip was uneventful.

Halfway through November the order came for the hospital to close to new admissions. Twelve hours later the order was rescinded and the hospital was ordered to take a number of new patients, the majority of which were suffering from Venereal Disease infections.

At this point Rose Daniels commented that:

"The atmosphere is more like a civilian hospital because the type of illnesses requires active treatment over a short period of time – no convalescence, thus immediate return to their unit" (231st A.R.C. Archives).

By the end of November the patient population was about forty and a number of the medical personnel were returned to the States. The hospital was finally closed on 31 December 1945.

Part Three:

Wood Farm – Plant 4176

Chapter 14

SHAKE DOWN

The 55th General Hospital, under the command of Colonel Charles C.Gill, arrived at Plant 4176, Wood Farm at the end of March 1944. The hospital had been activated in May 1943 at Camp Joseph T.Robinson, Little Rock, Arkansas. By August 1943 all of the enlisted personnel had arrived at the camp and training programmes commenced. By the end of January 1944 the remainder of the officers and nurses had arrived and the outfit was brought to full strength. At the beginning of February five Red Cross girls joined the unit. While at Camp Robinson the 55th ran the station hospital for personnel on the base.

The personnel were also involved in field training. The nurses went on a two day bivouac which involved marching seven miles, engaging in simulated battles and solving typical field problems. The challenges included tent pitching, compass reading and operating under blackout conditions. During the two days the entire unit lived on C. Rations.

In the middle of February the unit left Arkansas and travelled to the staging camp of Camp Myles, Massachusetts where they underwent more field training.

From Massachusetts the unit travelled to the Port of Embarkation to be shipped overseas to the United Kingdom. On March 9 the unit arrived in the U.K. After spending a short time at the staging hospital in Llandudno the unit travelled to Malvern.

The hospital at Wood Farm had been built on a section of the Worcestershire Golf Course which had been established in 1927 when it had moved from Malvern Common. In the early part of the war half of the course had been acquired for growing crops of beans and wheat, thus reducing it to a nine hole course. In 1943 the land was requisitioned to build a hospital to cater for injured troops from the forthcoming invasion of the continent.

British contractors were hired to build the hospital. The electric wiring of the camp was carried out by the Worcester firm of Able and Smith. Malcolm Mason, who was 16 at the time, remembers being contracted to work there:

NURSES OF 55th GO ON BIVOUAC

Nurses of the 55th General Hospital went on a two-day bivouac this w e e k, marching seven miles to the bivouac area, and engaging in simulated battle tactics and t y p i c a l field problems.

Work in the field, directed by Lt. John Knight, p l a n s and training officer, included various problems of combat activity —tent pitching, compass reading, and operating under blackout conditions. The nurses, comprising the entire unit from the hospital, subsisted on C rations during the problem. Lt. Bernice Hoare is chief nurse of the 55th General Hospital unit.

——o——

Army nurses in training at Ft. Devens, Mass., scoop foxholes out of the snow, using mess-kits as implements.
(International Photo)

ARMY'S MAIDS OF MERCY FACING UP TO THE RIGORS OF WAR

A burning tank in foreground provides battle atmosphere for Army nurses, marching along the sky-line in deep snow at Ft. Devens, Mass. They undergo four weeks of training before being sent out to care for the sick and the wounded. Now see the picture below. . .
(International Photo)

Press cutting from Massachusetts newspaper describing
55th General Hospital nurses' training (M. Reeves).

"When I went for a job I was given a green card and told to report to Wood Farm. ... I had the option of paying a shilling a day for bed and board which I did. They were very friendly and I was far better off than living at home. There were five of us in a hut just below the clubhouse. We ate in a canteen with the Americans and lived like Lords. I had clothes given to me. The Americans were very generous."

Malcolm recalls that his wages were half a crown (12p) an hour.

Aerial view of Wood Farm hospital site (English Heritage).

Top: Hospital taken from the Malvern Hills (M. Reeves). Bottom: View of the hospital taken from the West looking downhill and towards the East. On the North side there is a parking lot for visitors' vehicles. The first building is the patient's Mess Hall and next to it is the Recreation Building. On the South side the first long building is the Laboratory and next to it is the H.Q. Building which faces the Receiving Office. Farther down hill, in the centre of the picture, is the Operating Room. The shorter buildings are the P.X., Post Office and Barber shop. The 2 storey building is the Steam Plant which supplied steam for the Operating Rooms and the Central supply (55th General Hospital Archives).

The site at Wood Farm had a position a little higher than the other hospitals on the slope leading to Malvern Ridge whose highest point is 1,395 feet above sea level. Commenting on the setting of the hospital Colonel Gill wrote:

The view out over the valley below and across to the Bredon Hills was fully as beautiful and impressive as that of the steep ridge to the West which towered above (55th General Hospital Archives).

The hospital was divided into four areas. The main part was further subdivided into four subdivisions known as 'ramps'. Ramp A was located at the north eastern corner and was composed of fourteen wards and two accompanying ramps, one leading to two isolation wards and the other to a group of three wards and a small mess hall intended for patients with genitor-urinary complaints or venereal disease. It was soon determined that this elaborate set up was unnecessary for genitor-urinary patients and a decision was made to convert the five treatment rooms and offices into an auxiliary surgical set up. This meant that as many as 60 operations could be carried out in one day with twelve operating tables being used simultaneously.

Ramp B was located in the centre of the hospital and consisted of six wards and an operating room connected by an enclosed corridor. The operating room was located at the centre of the cluster of buildings and was used as a

Left: Orientation Maps in front of entrance to operating room.
The 2 storey building at the back of the officers is the Steam Plant
(55th General Hospital Archives). Right: Same building (M. Reeves).

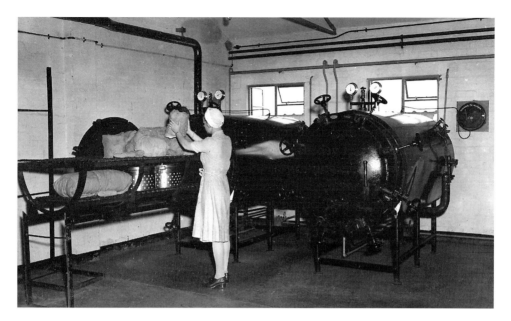

The two British made Autoclaves in the Sterilizing Room of the Central Supply Building. Both autoclaves experienced a number of mechanical problems but this did not prevent them from sterilising the equipment adequately (55th General Hospital Archives).

Dental Clinic; Eye, Ear, Nose and Throat clinic; X Ray; Physiotherapy; Laboratory; Central supply; Pharmacy; Post Exchange; Post Office and Barber Shop. Ramp G was located at the south-eastern corner and consisted of fourteen wards.

The second area, located directly West of Ramp B, was an administration area and consisted of Recreation Hall, Patients Mess Hall, Receiving Office and Headquarters. The third site included the living quarters and covered a wide area. The nurses living quarters were located in the north-western corner directly above Ramp A. The quarters for enlisted personnel were located between these two sites but higher up the hill. The fourth area ran parallel to the enlisted men's quarters and comprised a group of buildings which included the warehouse, chapel, fire station, motor pool with parking space and fields for recreational activities.

An advance party of the 55th had preceded the main group and on arrival the men of the party had assisted the British contractors to clean up huts, put up beds and organise the use of a mess hall. Even so when the main bulk of the unit arrived there was still much to do. For the next month the hospital personnel, clothed in fatigue uniforms, set to work cleaning and preparing buildings, unpacking supplies and landscaping the grounds.

The Utility Section of the 55th had come prepared to make some of the fixtures and fittings for the buildings. Back in the U.S. they had constructed packing cases in such a manner that they could be utilised for other purposes. They also wired the electric motors they had brought over so that they would work on the 220 volt current that the U.K. used at that time.

More wood was needed so several truckloads of lumber were collected from depots in the U.K. where machinery had arrived in crates. These were carefully taken apart and stored ready for the carpentry shop to use for shelves, stands, filing cabinets and chests.

One difficulty the Utility Department encountered was that beds and tables were sinking into the relatively soft pitch mastic floors. The problem was solved by cutting 5,000 small wooden blocks four inch square and two inches thick. In the centre a 1¼ inch hole was drilled to accommodate the feet of the furniture. The blocks were painted to match the floor.

Another problem for the Utility Department was the poor state of the tables to be used in the offices, mess halls and wards. They had been stacked outside for several months and it was necessary for the men to wash, scrape, sand and varnish them before they could be placed in the buildings.

The Utility Department also found that several of the buildings were not suitably equipped. The X-Ray Department had all of its permanent X-Ray machines installed in one room. This meant that when a fluoroscopic examination was being carried out no pictures could be taken. A brick wall, a foot thick and covered with barium plaster, was constructed between the fluoroscopic unit and the other units dividing the space into two separate rooms.

The men also constructed a waiting room for the Laboratory Section by building a wall across the room, thus separating the actual laboratory from the patients waiting. This served the dual purpose of preventing the laboratory workers from being disturbed each time someone entered the room and also hid from the view of the patients the many strange looking pieces of apparatus. A window was incorporated into the wall at a height which permitted the patients coming in for a blood count or venapuncture to sit on a chair, put his arm though the window and have the laboratory attendant obtain the necessary specimen.

The Dental Department found the Dental Clinic unfinished on their arrival but decided that this was a situation that they could use to their advantage as it gave them the opportunity to incorporate several features into the building which it would have been difficult to do once the construction was completed.

Nurses' Nissen huts (M. Reeves).

Fortunately the Dental personnel included men with training as sheet metal workers, carpenters, mechanics and electronics. Cabinets were constructed, adjustable foot rests and other items were made, which added to the efficiency of the operation. A nearby ordnance unit constructed the denture flasks, flask presses, a clasp surveyor and various chucks for the lathes. Other equipment procured included specialised tools used in the construction of artificial eyes.

The Mess Department also found it necessary to make a number of adaptations to the messing arrangements as they existed on the arrival of the unit. Previously, at Camp Robinson, the department had been accustomed to running three messes, two for enlisted personnel and one for officers. At Wood Farm there were six separate kitchens for the sixty six men to work in.

The mess for the enlisted personnel was in the enlisted area. The one for male officers had a kitchen combined with two large rooms, one for use as a dining hall, the other for a sitting room. The Nurses' Mess Hall was similar to the officer's but larger so it was decided to combine the male officers and nurses in the Nurses Mess Hall. The Patients Mess had two dining rooms, each seating 200 people, and a kitchen large enough to prepare food for the entire patient population. There were two smaller messes which could be operated for Officer and V.D. Patients.

During the first few weeks it was necessary for the Detachment to utilise the patient's messing

Nurse, Margaret Masterton with Malvern Hills behind her (M. Reeves).

facilities while the workmen completed the construction of the Detachment Mess. On completion it was necessary for the building to be used by two to three hundred British workers during the last month of construction. The building was turned over to the unit only a few days before the first patients were received at the hospital.

From their arrival at Wood Farm at the end of March the hospital personnel had one month to settle into their roles and become accustomed to working in an overseas general hospital. During this month the personnel made visits to other hospitals in the area to study methods already in use and notes were made of procedures that would work well at Wood Farm. They also spent time in training.

At Camp Robinson the unit had run the station hospital which was considerably smaller and dealt only with illnesses and training accidents encountered at the base. At Wood Farm the 55th would be running a larger general hospital and dealing with a large number of patients with combat injuries. As Colonel Gill writes in his report:

"This month of 'shake down' was a life saver figuratively for our organisation and literally for the patients who were about to arrive"(55th General Hospital Archives).

At the end of April the hospital was designated a 'Neuro Surgical Centre'. Neurosurgery focuses on treating the central, peripheral nervous system and spinal column.

The hospital was officially opened for patients at the end of April, the first three arriving on 7 May when the first operation was performed. The Pharmacy, X-Ray, Laboratory and Operating Rooms were still only functioning in a limited manner at this point because of the state of the buildings. When surgery took place it was necessary for the civilian electrician, Wally Pearson to be on stand by in case of electrical failure.

Chapter 15

TRAINLOADS OF PATIENTS

On 12 June two trains arrived at Malvern Wells Station carrying casualties from France for the 55th. One came early in the morning and the other late at night.

In the previous month the unit had spent some time observing other units loading and unloading trains and devised a plan for carrying out this procedure. The plan needed to take into consideration the details of the hospital set up, roads, unloading points and accessibility to the two railway stations, one on the Great Western Railway (G.W.R.) and one on the London Midland Scottish Railway (L.M.S.) line.

The hospital would be notified first by telephone to inform the personnel of the arrival of the train and the numbers of litter and ambulatory patients. If there were litter patients the hospital would need to know which type of train they were travelling on. Hospital trains with racks presented little problem to those unloading the train as the litters could be lifted off the rack in the train and then fitted directly onto the fittings in the ambulance. One such train carrying 230 stretchers and 70 ambulatory cases was unloaded in just over three minutes by the personnel of the 55th.

However the trains fitted with bunks beds in vertical series of threes gave the patients a more comfortable journey. When the patients arrived on this type of train it was necessary to lift the patient out of bed and onto a stretcher and then lift him out of the train and into the ambulance. The hospital had the use of both American and British stretchers, American and British wheeled stretcher carriers and British and American ambulances. Unfortunately American stretchers would not fit the British equipment and vice versa. The men soon found that both types of equipment had their own peculiarities and it was necessary to practise handling both types.

Once the hospital had been informed that the train was on its way the Receiving Officers, accompanied by several doctors would meet the train several stops before Malvern Wells. Once the officers were on board they would interview the patients to discover the type of injuries sustained and the type of treatment needed. Once this was ascertained a coloured tag was tied

Top: Malvern Wells G.W.R. Station at top of Peachfield Road. Station Master's house is in centre of picture. (P. Evans). Bottom: South view from Malvern Wells G.W.R. Station. Siding on right is where patients were unloaded from U.S. Army hospital trains. (P. Evans).

Left: G.I. with Station Master's daughters at Malvern Wells G.W.R. Station (D. Parkes). Right: Station Master at Malvern Wells G.W.R. Station (D. Parkes).

to the patient which would determine which ramp (A, B or C) he should be directed to. Notes were made on any patients in critical condition and the approximate number needing penicillin, transfusions or immediate surgery. The Chaplain from the 55th and members of the Red Cross unit also boarded the train early. The Red Cross girls were able to greet each patient and answer the men's questions about the hospital and England generally. They also distributed cigarettes, matches and gum.

In the meantime, back at Wood Farm, a group of officers and about 75 men collected any extra equipment needed from the depot. This would include litters, blankets, linen and food for replenishing the larder on the train. Arrangements could be made to 'borrow' ambulances from the other nearby hospitals if necessary. Occasionally buses with a seating capacity of thirty were available for ambulatory patients. When the train stopped at the platform ambulatory men were guided off the train and sent by bus to the hospital where they could get a hot meal and be settled in their ward. Litter patients could then be unloaded from the train and loaded onto the ambulance that would take them to the appropriate ramp.

To avoid traffic congestion caused by ambulances leaving the hospital while others were arriving, a one way system was devised. After gaining permission from the farmer a short addition to the concrete runway was constructed, which took it onto the private road at Warren Farm.

Once at the hospital patients were bathed, shaved, ate and then slept. Doctors made ward rounds and classified the patients into groups depending on the urgency of the surgery, transfusions or other treatments. When patients arrived by the trainload it would be common to see transfusions of blood or plasma commenced before the last of the litter cases was wheeled onto the ward.

At first new patients were evenly distributed through the hospital. However it was found that when the hospital was busy this system had some drawbacks, principally because the scattering of patients throughout the hospital area made it difficult for the Chiefs of Services to keep track of all their patients when they were on several different wards. To improve this situation the procedure was altered so that when a trainload of patients were expected a few wards were emptied completely, then designated temporarily for various surgical specialities. This simplified the supervision of new arrivals because the doctor had all of his new patients together. However it did place a considerable burden of nursing care on the receiving wards because of the number of new patients.

It was necessary for the Laboratory Department to establish a system for handling large convoys of patients. It devised a system with three ratings: emergency, urgent and routine. 'Emergency' requests were to be dealt with as speedily as possible, 'Urgent' requests were accomplished during the same day while 'Routine' requests were dealt with as soon as all the other priority requests had been completed.

The Laboratory Department also decided that on admission all patients would have a complete blood count, urinalysis and Kuhn test. This was to prove of value as a number of conditions were found which otherwise may not have been detected.

The Anaesthesia Department also found it necessary to establish procedures with regard to giving

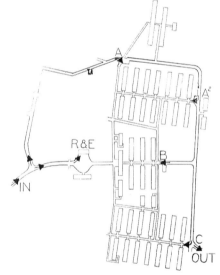

Diagram showing one way system for ambulances arriving at and leaving Wood Farm. Ambulances enter through the main gate at the southwest corner of the post. A series of Hospital Police directs them onward to the correct unloading point (55th General Hospital Archives).

Top: Ambulance backed up to the Receiving and Evacuation Office where ambulatory patients are detrucking. Clerks at the R&E are inspecting their records. The covered entranceway was constructed by the Utility Department to afford protection to patients being unloaded in the rain (55th General Hospital Archives). Bottom left: Personnel from the 55th loading patients into ambulances from Malvern Wells L.M.S. Station. Four ambulances are backed up to receive the litter patients being removed from three cars. An officer directs the filling of ambulances, selecting for each only those destined for one ramp. The dispatcher of the Motor Pool controls the shuttling of ambulances from the reserve line to the loading point and tells the driver the unloading point in the hospital area selected for his load (55th General Hospital Archives). Bottom right: Attendants at the extreme left are wheeling a patient to his ward. Another patient has been placed on the wheeled litter carrier and is about to be taken to the ward designated by the coloured tag placed on him during the latter part of the train journey (55th General Hospital Archives).

Unloading a patient on the upper end of Ramp A (55th General Hospital Archives).

anaesthesia to those awaiting operations. It was found to be most effective if the patient was given medication before bedtime and repeated at 6 a.m. This:

" *... diminished the nursing problem on the ward in that the patient slept through the eating hours and was not likely to eat or drink at that time. The patient was not excited by the other patients' constant chattering and its accompanying 'horse play' such as asking the patient going to the operating room what kind of casket he would like to have and what are his favourite flowers*" *(55th General Hospital Archives)*.

Just before the patient left the ward for the operating theatre, morphine and atrophine was administered.

One of the patients arriving at Wood Farm on 12 June amongst the first trainload of patients was Shirley S. Hartline. He was a member of G. Company, 325th Glider Infantry Regiment, 82nd Airborne Division. In the early hours of June 7 he had been flown by glider from England to France. The glider was towed by a C47 and escorted by P38 Lightnings and Spitfires. Shirley remembers looking down at the English Channel as they flew over it and seeing ships in every direction, as far as the eye could see. The glider flew about five or six miles inland to Chef du Pont where the landing zone was located. Unfortunately the larger field that the glider was intended to land in was staked with posts to prevent glider landings so it was necessary to land in one of the smaller fields.

The C47 cut the glider loose and preparations were made for the landing. Shirley tightened his seatbelt and held his rifle diagonally across his body. The pilot put on full brakes but due to the incline of the field and wetness of the grass the glider didn't slow down as much as it should have done. The pilot aimed to steer the glider between two large trees in the hedgerow but the right wing caught the wing of a glider that had hit the hedgerow earlier. When Shirley came to he found himself on the other side of the hedge still clutching his rifle. The impact had ejected him out of the glider and killed the co-pilot and eight of his colleagues including the Platoon Leader, Lieutenant Robert Maxwell, who

Nurse Margaret Masterton on night duty (M. Reeves).

was standing in the doorway of the aircraft as it came into land. The pilot, who was lying on the ground near Shirley, had also survived the impact although Shirley needed to give him a shot of morphine because of his injuries.

After the landing the men were ordered to assemble, only 37 men out of a company of 128 were accounted for. Shirley had sustained some minor injuries from the impact of the glider landing. He remembers:

"I was bruised from the landing and probably had concussion, as my nose started bleeding. I had grazed my left hip badly and went to an aid station to get it taken care of, but before I could see a medic we were told to return to our company. They told us to 'fix bayonets' for we were to go on a night attack. We searched all night but did not make contact with the Germans."

On 9th June the men were ordered to attack at 0400 hours. The Battalion's objective was to reach La Ham and to get there it was necessary to cross La Fiere Causeway. The men advanced up the hill to a hedgerow but when they crossed over the hedgerow they exposed themselves to the cross fire of the Germans in the next hedgerow. Shirley had only gone a few feet when a mortar shell hit the ground between him and his comrade. As the mortar exploded Shirley hit the ground and avoided injury. He got up and

Tally sheet signed by supply officer, Robert Wasley (M. Reeves).

joined his comrade who was surprised to see him as he thought Shirley had been killed in the blast.

In the next field the unit was pinned down by machine gun and mortar fire and several were killed, including the Company Commander, Captain Irvin Bloom. A mortar shell hit the top of the tree Shirley was lying under and he was hit by shrapnel in his right leg and foot. He took the sulfa pills he had been given and bandaged his own wounds. He was pinned down under the heavy barrage for three hours. When the barrage eased up he attempted to make his way to the rear. He crawled along the back of the hedgerow until he came to a farmhouse where a French family looked after him. The wife gave him an egg with bread and a glass of wine and the husband, who had lost a leg in the First World War, gave him a small glass with clear liquid in. When he drank it he found it hard to catch his breath. This was his first introduction to Calvados.

At dusk two soldiers from the 505th Paratroop Regiment helped Shirley to the Field Aide Station. On the night of 10 June the wounded were loaded onto G.M.C. trucks which were equipped with eighteen stretchers, nine loaded at seat level and nine across the side boards on top. The truck took them to the shore where an L.S.T. was waiting to take them on board.

Just as the truck arrived a German plane flew at low altitude along the line of landing crafts being loaded. Fortunately no one was hurt. Apparently the medics had named the pilot 'Bed Check Charlie' as he made the pass over at the same time every night. It was necessary for the L.S.T. to wait for the next morning's tide before it could move off the shore. It took the men to a hospital ship which sailed to Southampton from where the patients were taken by train to the 55th General Hospital.

When Shirley had recovered enough he was able to visit some of his colleagues who were being treated in some of the other hospitals in Malvern. In September he was able to rejoin his unit. He found that the unit had not been relieved until they had spent 31 consecutive days in combat in France. When Shirley rejoined the unit he found that only one officer and five enlisted men from the original unit were still with the unit, the rest had been killed or wounded.

Staff Sergeant John Cramer arrived as a patient of the 55th later in the war. He was the Squad Leader of A Company Rifle Platoon, 310th Infantry, 78th Division. He sailed for Le Havre, Normandy in November 1944 and from here his unit travelled to Maastricht, Holland and through the Hurtgen Forest to Lammersdorf, Germany. The first real action the unit encountered was an attack toward the Siegfried Line on December 13.

Over the next few weeks the unit repelled several German attacks and went back on the attack on January 25. On February 6 John was

John Cramer and Calvin 'Slick Chic' Chilson (J. Cramer).

Picture of Motor Pool at 55th sent to John Cramer's parents by Bob Wasley (J. Cramer).

hit by shrapnel in the right groin and right hand in an artillery barrage at Schmidt in Germany. He was taken to the Battalion Aid Station in a jeep and then onto a field hospital where the dressing was changed. From here John was transported to a hospital in Liege, Belgium, where he was operated on and the shrapnel was removed from his groin. Next John was taken to Paris where he was given stitches and then sent by ship to England. At the end of February he arrived at 155th General Hospital at Blackmore Park, Malvern, where his stitches were removed.

One afternoon an officer from the 55th arrived at Blackmore Park to speak to him. The officer, Lieutenant Bob Wasley, knew John's father and he persuaded him to request a transfer to the 55th where he was Supply Officer.

When John had completed his treatment the doctor told him he could start walking short distances and then commence his rehabilitation. When John attempted to get out of his bed he found that he couldn't manage it by himself so a fellow patient helped him out of bed, supporting him as he walked as far as the bathroom and then left him there saying: 'You can walk back'. He did manage to walk back and that was the start of his rehabilitation. John finished rehabilitation on May 4 when he received seven days furlough and was then ordered to report to the 10th Replacement Depot in Lichfield, Staffordshire from where he travelled back to join his unit on occupation duty in Germany.

Chapter 16

RETURNING THE PATIENT TO DUTY

Prior to June 12th the hospital census was just under 200 but the two trains arriving in Malvern Wells on that day brought 500 more patients and two days later the census had reached nearly 1000. Between 12th June and 27th September 1944 eleven train loads of patients were received at the hospital thus making a total of 3094 patients received during four months. Some patients needing emergency treatment were transported by plane from the continent arriving at Pershore Airfield and then taken by ambulance to Wood Farm. During the period from June to September 1944 353 patients requiring neurosurgery were also transferred to Wood Farm from other hospitals in the 12th Hospital Centre.

It was soon found necessary to add ward tents to the ends of ward buildings to accommodate the extra patients. (Later, as the numbers decreased, some of the ward tents were left empty and the G.I.s used them for 'other' purposes. Ray Peterson remembers that girlfriends would sometimes be 'entertained' there.)

Because the 55th was a neurosurgery hospital the surgical department was particularly busy. There were a large number of amputations of limbs performed at the hospital. This was often due to the damage by trench foot and gangrene. Patient, John Cramer recalls seeing a doctor fitting a mirror to one of the patient's crutches so that he could see the stump of his leg where the foot had been amputated. John remembers the doctor remarking to the patient: "*That foot will never get cold again.*" A large mirror, six foot by three foot was purchased through the hospital fund and framed by the carpenter to aid amputees to improve their walking skills.

The neuropsychiatric section at the hospital also had a large number of patients admitted, many of these suffering from combat exhaustion. All psychiatric patients and the majority of the officer neuropsychiatric patients were admitted directly to the 96th General Hospital for psychiatric treatment. Therapy for neuropsychiatric patients at Wood Farm consisted of sedation, insulin, individual and group psychotherapy, exercise and sports. Out of the 100 combat exhaustion patients treated by this section only a small number were returned to the U.S. Most were recommended for non-combat duty.

Patients arriving at Pershore airfield (55th General Hospital Archives).

In the first month after the hospital opened the Venereal Disease and Dermatalogic Diseases section had a large number of patients as the 55th was serving as station hospital for white and black troops stationed in the vicinity. From the first trainload this section received sixteen patients but thereafter its quota did not exceed six per train and very few of these were Venereal Disease cases. The dermatological conditions encountered were chiefly impetigo and fungal infections often complicated by secondary infections. This department also treated patients in the surgical section who had skin diseases.

Because of the large number of patients admitted the Mess Department found that their facilities were stretched. Colonel Gill commented that the work in the patients mess resembled at times a:

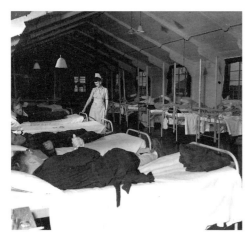
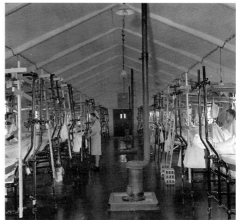
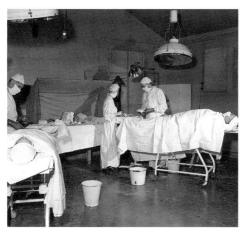
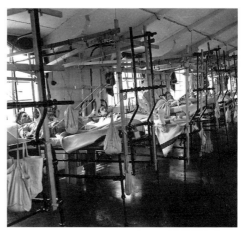

Top left: Amputation Ward (55th General Hospital Archives). Bottom left: Operating Room designed for two operating tables in simultaneous use. The overhead lights were found to be inadequate and were supplemented with portable lamps. Top right and bottom right: Wards at 55th General Hospital (55th General Hospital Archives).

" ... *five ring circus, extremely busy, not very efficient and a constant worry"* (55th General Hospital Archives).

Cooks and assistants started their shift at noontime and usually worked until ten or eleven o'clock at night before the place was tidied up after the evening meal. A small number of convalescent patients also worked in the kitchens as part of their rehabilitation.

Because of the large numbers to be catered for it was necessary for the mess staff to adjust their methods of serving. The seating capacity of the two dining rooms was 400 but the number of ambulatory patients was around 800. The 55th decided to introduce a method they'd seen work at one of the nearby hospitals. Two serving lines were established, first the crippled patients who needed help were served then the ambulatory patients who would eat their meal and carry their soiled utensils to the window of the dishwashing room where the waste particles were scraped off, the trays rinsed and sent through the dishwashing machine. Over a period of weeks the Mess department got to the point where 700 people in the mess halls could be served in 40 minutes. At the same time meals were placed in containers on food carts and sent out for 600-700 patients on the wards.

When the numbers of patients increased it was found that there were not enough compartmental trays to serve patients on the wards and those in the Mess Hall. Consequently individuals who finished first had their trays quickly removed, washed and used again. In the later part of June trays were used and washed three times during each meal. Field ranges were brought into provide additional cooking facilities and hot water. Eventually a dishwashing machine was installed, thus saving manpower.

Another problem to be addressed by the Mess Department was hygiene, or lack of it. In order to teach the importance of dealing with bacteria the laboratory service prepared demonstrations for mess personnel. Using

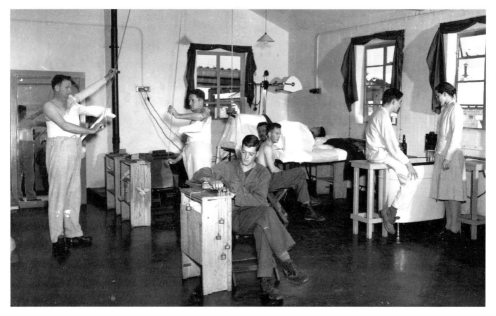

Main room of Physical Therapy Department (55th General Hospital Archives).

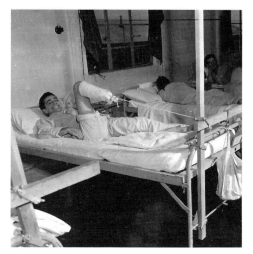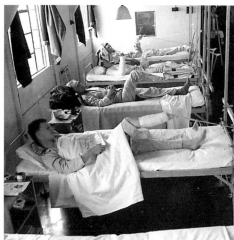

Exercises for amputees (55th General Hospital Archives).

microscopes men were shown the colony counts taken from their finger prints left on dishes that had been passed through the steam of the dishwashing machine. The men took heed of the demonstration and were soon putting germ free dishes on the dining tables.

An important part of the treatment of patients at the 55th was Physical Therapy and Rehabilitation. Lilian Seidler, Assistant Field Director of the Red Cross unit attached to the 55th, defines the aim of the Rehabilitation Programme in the 55th General Hospital:

"The Rehabilitation Programme is primarily concerned with returning a patient to duty in the best possible condition, mental and physical. Throughout a soldiers entire hospitalisation period all persons concerned with the patients care must keep this in view" (55th A.R.C. Archives).

The American Red Cross participated in the Rehabilitation Programme. As Lilian Seidler comments:

"Red Cross workers in their daily ward rounds and in their frequent contact with the patient population can do much to foster a spirit of progress and interest in the return to duty rather that fostering a spirit of hopelessness and regression. The Red Cross workers, perhaps more than others, can offer sympathy without allowing a patient to become dependent or despondent" (A.R.C.55th Archives).

Upon arrival at Wood Farm, Medical Officers visited rehabilitation centres and rehabilitation sections of hospitals in the area to gain a comprehensive picture of the requirements for this department. As soon as the first patients arrived the Physical Therapy Department put into place a system of exercises for those on orthopaedic wards. Even bed patients were encouraged to exercise the shoulders and fingers. The emphasis was placed on 'active exercise' although there were facilities for massage and infra red treatment when required. Early exercise was advocated, mild active motion, carefully supervised, was commenced as soon as doctors permitted it and usually before injuries were fully healed.

Colonel Gill wanted the rehabilitation patients to take responsibility for their own progress and states in his report that:

"Each was encouraged to realise that he had to work for his own cure" (55th General Hospital Archives).

A medical ward was vacated and transferred into a gymnasium. Beds were removed and utilised for double decking in other buildings. Lumber was obtained from a nearby depot and the men in the programme constructed their own equipment. By the end of September 1944 the gymnasium was fully equipped and frequently used as poor weather often prevented an outside drill.

The Rehabilitation Patients were permitted privileges that the other patients didn't have. They were given passes more frequently and for a longer duration. They were not placed on labour details except those directly appertaining to their barracks area and the construction of facilities for their use.

Malcolm Mason remembers that rehabilitation patients were often put on the wood pile to chop wood for the stoves in their barracks. One of the men he watched chopping wood was a large man of Native American origin. Malcolm

Outdoor exercises for general reconditioning (55th General Hospital Archives).

Rehabilitation Class at exercise. The leader is a graduate of the school at the 307th Station Hospital (55th General Hospital Archives).

recalls that he was often in trouble as he regularly used to climb over the stile on the boundary of the camp and walk to the Hornyold Arms for a drink.

Some mental and educational training was also given to the rehabilitation patients in the form of group discussions and talks on combat subjects in which the class leader was an officer patient with combat experience. The paratroopers were gathered together for discussions conducted by paratroop officers.

By September 1944 the Rehabilitation Programme was being run by a patient group. They were responsible for their own projects which included putting up a ward tent for the Red Cross to use as an additional games room and helping to make improvements to the Red Cross building. In October the Red Cross building was completely decorated with the assistance of the men in the Rehabilitation Programme. Dorothy Maquire, the Recreation Worker, describes the finished effect:

"During this face lifting period it was necessary to curtail activities in the building for a day and a half. Remarks made by 'peeping toms' such as – 'What is a powder

Outdoor gymnasium equipment, installed by patients of the Rehabilitation Group (55th General Hospital Archives).

room?', 'Looks like a Gin Mill' while the renovation was taking place made the staff a little dubious of the trust they had placed in the patient chosen as interior decorator."

The final effect was described:

"The two side walls of the building were painted an indescribable rose pink and the two end walls a grey. Signal red woodwork completed the basic colour scheme. Blackout curtains were replaced by gay coloured draw curtains and red cornices. Slip covers were made for the furniture and pillows were scattered here and there. French posters secured through the British Council made gay pictures for the walls. The result of the whole redecoration has greatly improved the appearance and atmosphere of the buildings and both staff and patients are well pleased" (A.R.C. 55th Archives).

Unfortunately this opinion was not shared by Mrs Alice Pearson, the Red Cross Field Director, when she visited the base in May 1945. She particularly noticed the:

" ... bad combination of color on the wall, paint and the curtains. The walls are painted a peculiar shade of salmon pink which is in severe conflict with the bright orange and red in the curtain material" (A.R.C. 55th Archives).

The Rehabilitation Group also built and equipped a larger and more efficient Hobby Workshop for the Red Cross. Five large, heavy woodwork tables complete with vices, a counter and shelves and several small craft tables were built. Additional tools and supplies were secured through a salvage depot and through the Red Cross. The workshop was used by members of the Rehabilitation Group for the construction of items needed in their programme such as filing cabinets, basket ball backstands, punching bag stands and hangers.

The Rehabilitation Group had their own baseball team known as the 'Purple Heart Cripples'. This team played several games against teams from other units in the vicinity. When playing away from home the group requested a Red Cross worker to accompany them. When playing at home refreshments to the team and their opponents were served in the Red Cross building.

When their treatment was completed patients were transferred to different destinations according to their needs. The hospital aimed to return as many as possible back to duty although it was necessary to transfer some patients back to hospitals dealing with different specialisms and a number were sent back to the U.S. either for further treatment or for discharge from the military due to their injuries.

Of the 3447 men admitted between July and September 1944, 2618 had completed their treatment by the end of September. Over a thousand were sent directly back to their units or to a Replacement Depot for reassignment. Another 550 were considered able to return to duty after suitable rehabilitation had been carried out. Of this number approximately five sixths were able to return to duty while the balance continued their treatment. Approximately 400 were transferred to other hospitals primarily for the purpose of making room for additional trainloads of patients. A small number of these men were British and French casualties who were transferred to hospitals operated by their own armies. 616 men were sent back to the U.S.

Activities at 307th Rehabilitation Hospital at Stoneleigh,
Warwickshire (U.S. Archives).

One of the patients, John Cramer, recalls that some of the patients would, understandably, try to avoid being sent back to duty. He remembers one who had completed his treatment but complained to the doctor that he was suffering from severe back pain. One evening the patient was playing ping pong when the doctor walked in. John recalls: 'Needless to say in about 15 minutes he was gone. I don't know where but probably back to the front.'

Between July and September 1944 152 patients were transferred to Rehabilitation Centres. The Commanding Officer from the 307th Rehabilitation Centre at Stoneleigh Park, Warwickshire sent a letter to Colonel Gill setting out the requirements for patients to be transferred there:

"We are equipped and prepared to take ambulatory patients who do not require a special diet, who do not have neuropsychiatric problems and whose physical status is such that they can be rehabilitated in the E.T.O. … Our program of rehabilitation embodies the plan of rendering the soldier physically fit for combat duty, returning him to an atmosphere of army life, reviving his military efficiency and the bolstering of his morale" (55th General Hospital Archives).

During the period July to September 1944 a group of 367 men were sent to the 77th Station Hospital at Bromsgrove for reconditioning and 37 officers were transferred to the 123rd Officers Reconditioning Hospital, also based at Bromsgrove.

Chapter 17

A MEDICALLY APPROVED
RECREATION PROGRAMME

The Red Cross unit attached to the 55th consisted of five girls who catered for the welfare and recreational needs of the patients. The function of the Recreation Department of the unit was:

" ... *primarily concerned with providing a medically approved recreation program for hospital patients. It also offers assistance in recreational activities that are conducted by the Special Service Officer and the Chaplains for hospital personnel*" *(ARC 55)*.

The Red Cross were given the use of the Recreational Building which, like a number of the buildings on site, was incomplete upon arrival of the unit. The girls asked the contractors to build partitions at one end of the buildings so that it could be divided into five small rooms to use as offices, store rooms and work rooms. The larger room was to be used as a lounge and was equipped with writing desks, easy chairs, tables, a radio phonograph and a piano. This room also housed a ping pong table that had been loaned by a British family and a snooker table. A fire place was built in the centre of one of the walls.

The Assistant Field Director, Lilian Seidler, found that using the Recreation Building for Red Cross activities caused some conflict with the Special Service personnel on the post as, if the Red Cross used the building exclusively, there was no provision for other entertainment activities such as movies, lectures, USO shows and the like. In May two movies and a concert were held in the Recreation Hall which necessitated moving all the Red Cross equipment into the smaller rooms and then moving it back the next day.

Lilian Seidler felt that the Red Cross had the lowest priority out of the groups at Wood Farm for equipment and building work. She noticed that the fire place in the Red Cross building was constructed last, after the ones in the officers club and male and female Officers' Day Rooms. She also complained that:

"*We find ourselves with a building which the army was to furnish but no furniture of any sort was available for our use. We were requested rather to assist in furnishing the Officer clubs and the Officer Patients Recreation Hall ... When generalized planning for initial distribution of supplies and essential equipment took place, Red Cross on this post was completely forgotten. Later, because of E.T.O. shortages, nothing was available for our use. We have had to fight, beg, borrow and steal each and every individual article we have been able to acquire. This has put us in an exceedingly difficult situation and has left us feeling that we have been constantly on the 'receiving' end and have been forced to beg for the essentials with which to produce and prove our worth"* (55th A.R.C. Archives).

By July the unit were established in their building and had received the equipment that was needed. By this time the hospital was full of patients and a full programme of recreational events was organised. During this month the unit put on an 'evening highlight' programme. A Fourth of July, horse race and card parties were some of the highlight events.

In April, meetings had taken place between members of the local Women's Volunteer Services and the Red Cross to establish what could be done to support the hospital's recreation programme. It was decided that the WVS should organise off post tours and visits of the patients and hospital personnel to British homes. This was appreciated, especially by the patients. Margaret Vanhoeff, the Staff Aide of the Red Cross unit reported about the visits:

"They are not only entertaining and educational, they are not only a way of getting the patients out of the hospital, but they are often the first step back into civilian social life. For example many of the ambulatory patients that attend are N.P. patients or those going back to the States. It adds much to their rehabilitation to meet older British people, see a beautiful home, learn its history, play with the children, milk the cows or look for deer. Many of the patients have a pretty hard time holding a dainty plate on one knee and a teacup on the other, but as the hosts have been unfailingly understanding and since there were always enough nervous ones to keep each other company nobody seemed to mind" (55th A.R.C. Archives).

Several large estates were visited. Dorothy Maguire, the Recreation Worker comments:

"It was interesting to watch the G.I.s examining famous antique china one moment and casually filling their blouses with apples 'lifted' from the hostess' garden a few

WELCOME HOME FUND DANCE

There was an Anglo-American atmosphere at the successful dance organised in aid of the Malvern Welcome Home Fund by the Malvern Chamber of Commerce on Friday week at the Winter Gardens. Major W. J. C. Kendall and many other supporters of the fund attended, and there was special interest in the presence of Lieut. E. Cleverley and Cpl. Donald Williams, until recently prisoners of war in Germany.

A non-stop programme of dances was played alternately by Billy Gammon's Band and the band of the 55th General Hospital of the U.S. Army. The Lancers was ably conducted by Mr. E. D. Bowman. Master Tony Hunt sang, accompanied by Billy Gammon's Band, and both he and an American soldier singing with the U.S. band, S/Sgt. Johnny Cooley, were well received.

There were gay floral table decorations, and a noticeable feature was that, with no more black-out to hamper ventilation, the usual "blue" air which has been so apparent at most large dances was conspicuous by its absence.

After a competition the dances played were alternately old-fashioned and modern, and included a barn dance.

The dance ended with a rousing quick-step to music by both bands. The Americans' band playing the "Star - spangled Banner" and Billy Gammons' playing "God Save the King," concluded the programme.

The Welcome Home Fund will benefit considerably by the event.

Malvern Gazette.

minutes later. The laughter and singing as we were homeward bound proved that the hot cup of tea and cordial hospitality of our hostesses had worked their charm" (55th A.R.C. Archives).

The W.V.S. also helped to arrange sightseeing tours. On Saturdays trips were taken to the Shakespeare Memorial Theatre at Stratford upon Avon. After the matinee, sightseeing trips were taken though the town to see Shakespeare's birthplace. The men could then have dinner at the Red Cross Service Club or at a restaurant.

The following year it was more difficult to arrange tours because of the lack of staff to cover them. Because the Red Cross staff were busy running activities on the post they gave other personnel, such as the Rehabilitation Officer Patients the responsibility of organising and accompanying the tours. Unfortunately an incident on one of the tours had occurred the day before Alice Pearson, the Red Cross Field Director, came to inspect the Red Cross activities. In her report she stated that the trip:

" ... had not proved altogether successful since the officer patient had not checked the roll too carefully and one of the patients failed to return with the tour" (55th A.R.C. Archives).

Another form of recreation available in the locality was golf. One section of the Worcestershire Golf Course still remained and so a number of the male personnel spent off duty time there. Terry Cole, who was a youngster at the time, remembers caddying for the Americans in return for chewing gum.

Movies were shown to the patients as part of the recreation programme but there was only one projector on the post which the Red Cross and Special Service shared. In September 1944 the problems over the sharing of the projector were solved by the intervention of the Red Cross Field Supervisor who suggested that the Special Service should use the projector to show movies and the Red Cross could make better use of their time supervising other activities. The Special Service Officer agreed to this and stated that he would ensure that movies were also shown on the wards to bed patients but Dorothy Maguire noted in the Red Cross report that:

"Unfortunately this does not occur frequently due to lack of personnel and the constant use of the machine in the theatre" (55th A.R.C. Archives).

Later the Red Cross adapted the large coal bin on the site into a theatre to show movies. This was aptly named 'The Coal Bin Theatre' and was also used for the presentation of other Red Cross entertainment.

From July the Red Cross organised recreational activities on the wards. On dull days the theatrical make up set was taken around the wards and contests were conducted in which patients were made up as various characters e.g.

glamour girl, Hill-Billy or gangster. The patients also enjoyed bingo, magic games and auction games on the wards.

Some crafts could be carried out on the wards. In September an elephant modelling contest using plasticine was held on Ramp C. The winning elephants were displayed throughout the wards. One of the patients that had been an art and skills teacher in civilian life gave the girls a seven day course in the rudiments of crafts and materials. Each member of the staff spent an hour and a half of her own time each day learning leather craft, clay modelling, papier mache, painting, block printing and weaving. The girls found that this gave them more confidence when teaching the skills to the patients.

One craft that was particularly popular with the patients was the making of life masks. Dorothy Maguire describes the process:

"A negative mould is made of the face with plaster of paris and a positive mould with wet clay is made from the negative mould. The mask is then finished by sculpturing done on the more detailed features and painting the finished product … it is indeed amusing to witness several patients flat on their back on the floor with two straws protruding from their nostrils and their faces covered with plaster. They lie perfectly still while the plaster is setting in order not to crack it. Another group sits concurrently in front of mirrors alternating a glance in the mirrors with a stroke of a sculpturing tool on their image in clay" (55th A.R.C. Archives).

In September 1944 two clubs opened in Malvern for the use of G.I.s. The first was a British-American club called 'The Welcome Club'. This was organised by the W.V.S. and was to serve as a recreation place for all military personnel. It consisted of a large and small games room. Once a week a discussion group was held at the club, one of the Red Cross staff would accompany a group of patients to the meeting.

The other club was the 'Doughnut Dugout' run by the Red Cross. In September the official opening featured the dance band from the 55th. The Mess Hall of the 55th made two huge cakes while the Red Cross workers at the Doughnut Dugout supplied the coffee. All of the hospitals in the area participated in the preparations for this event by choosing lots for the individual rooms and then decorating them. Patients helped with the decorating, painting the hospitals crest, Allied Nations flags and pictures of the Rehabilitation Programme. The 55th room won second prize. The 55th Dance Band also played at a dance organised in aid of the Malvern Welcome Home fund

In their off duty time the personnel from Wood Farm frequented several of the local pubs. Dennis Cottrell remembers that every evening officers from Wood Farm would visit the Westminster Arms Hotel in West Malvern. The hotel had a dance floor which it was Dennis' job to polish. The proprietor of the hotel had lost her husband early in the war and was very friendly with one of the officers. Dennis used to clean his car for him for seven shillings and sixpence.

Once the trainloads of patients started arriving on the post the case load for the Red Cross started growing. In June there were 64 cases, by September this had grown to 566. The increase was primarily due to an increase in loans to tide patients over until their pay caught up with them. The Red Cross policy was to attempt to keep loans to a minimum so girls would give out rations, haircuts, stamps and send cables for the patients to prevent the men from running in to debt. However as Lilian Seidler wrote:

"These men will be returning to combat and wish to enjoy what little freedom they may have before they return to the front. It has been our feeling that they are entitled to a small loan" (55th A.R.C. Archives).

As the hospital filled with casualties case work problems assumed a new importance, and were of a different nature to those dealt with previously. Numerous requests for welfare reports poured in as families learnt that their loved ones had been wounded. Entire wards were made up of amputation cases, each of whom needed reassurance and interpretation of disabilities:

"The fear of returning home and even greater fear of returning to battle had to be met over and over again" (55th A.R.C. Archives).

As Christmas approached the Red Cross found themselves very busy. This was partly due to a change of staffing. At the end of November, Assistant Field Director, Lilian Seidler was replaced by Mary Jean Clark. Apparently Lilian had caused some problems within the unit which the Field Supervisor, Alice Pearson, commented on in her report made in May 1945.

Over the Christmas period a number of activities were planned. Special Service provided each ward with a tree and also provided large trees for the mess halls and clubs. The Red Cross provided some tree decorations and patients made the rest. Broken test tubes were converted to attractive glass ornaments in the hobby shop. Just before Christmas children from a neighbouring school came to present a play which was enjoyed by all the patients.

The hospital also helped to provide a party for youngsters in the Link Top area at Trinity Hall, which was reported in the newspaper. Irene Carpenter, nee Clee, who was at the party, remembers that the main entertainment at the party was a conjurer. There were sandwiches, jellies and small treacle tarts to eat. Irene's mother and grandmother made toffee apples with the apples from the tree in their garden. Irene also remembers that the Americans from the area would often give the local children fruit and biscuits to take to

Irene Carpenter and friends at Link Top Christmas party. (I. Carpenter).

school. She recalls that the biscuits were so hard that they were inedible and she would save them to break up and give to the chickens at night. Irene remembers that a number of families from Link Top befriended the G.I.s and treated them like one of the family.

On Christmas Eve there was a Christmas party in the Red Cross Building when gifts were given to all the ambulatory patients. During that evening Santas and Mrs Santas in costumes were out on the wards hanging stockings on the beds, supposedly while the patients slept. On Boxing Day the hospital personnel was invited to the Red Cross building for 'Open House'. The Mess Hall provided refreshments and an informal evening was spent singing, playing snooker, ping pong and cards and chatting by the fireside.

At the beginning of 1945 a Volunteer Programme was inaugurated at the 55th. A programme had already been organised the previous September when Lilian Seidler was the A.F.D. Applications had been made by the local people to participate in the programme and forms had been completed. Unfortunately Colonel Gill, who had originally given permission for the Volunteer programme, later rescinded the decision pending reinterpretation of military approval of the use of civilians on hospital wards. At the end of 1944 the Colonel gave his approval to the programme so it was necessary to check if the original applicants were still available. By the end of January several women had been telephoned and appointments made for interviews. By the beginning of February six girls in their new uniforms were based in

Nurse, Margaret Masterton and colleagues (M. Reeves).

the Red Cross building for three to four hours a week distributing matches, writing paper, and games and wrapping paper to the patients. They were also equipped with a sewing kit to mend for the patients or to help the patients with their own mending.

The main Red Cross activity organised for March 1945 was the Spring Carnival. This was planned as a combined opening and dedication of the new hut, a large building easily converted into a room for fairly large parties. The use of the extra building meant that the main building could be free at least once a week for the use of the enlisted men of the hospital detachment. The Spring Carnival was organised by one of the patient civilian employees and some of the detachment offered their services for the evening and several patients who had travelled with a circus or carnival ran the various gambling gadgets. One of these featured a large picture of Hitler with a small hole in his hat through which cracked ping pong balls were thrown.

Eunice Matheson, the new Recreation Worker, described the nosiest game which was called 'See the Mousie Run':

"A board game about 30" square had sixteen holes around the outside with tin cans fitting underneath. Cheese was placed in each can and several white mice were brought over from the laboratory. Bets were placed on each hole and a mouse was turned loose in the middle of the board. The game was made exciting by fifteen men yelling 'No!' This bewildered the mouse and he ran from hole to hole before making up his mind just where he wanted to go" (55th A.R.C. Archives).

The day after the carnival a patient who had bet all of his hair that the ring toss he made wouldn't go over came in with his head shaved.

In May V.E. Day was celebrated by the personnel of the hospital. Mary Jean Clark describes the patient's reaction to the news:

"Throughout the days of the 7th and 8th of May the patients eagerly listened to the radio. Their feelings of relief that the fighting was finished here were colored by the knowledge that the fighting was still going on elsewhere. They did not lose sight of the fact that they still did not know what the future had in store for them" (55th *A.R.C. Archives*).

The Red Cross decided to organise an informal celebration of V.E. Day on the post as many of the patients and personnel had left to celebrate in Malvern and the local area. They decided on some informal singing with refreshments in the Red Cross Building. Each ward with non-ambulatory patients was given a tray decorated with handmade V.E. pennants and red and white paper. Packs of cigarettes, life savers, gum, matches and homemade fudge were placed in the tray.

On May 9th a notice was given to the hospital of its change and relocation to France. In June the hospital closed and reopened in Marmelon, France on July 1st.

Chapter 18

OVERSEAS WEDDINGS

Several weddings involving personnel from the 55th General Hospital took place during its time at Wood Farm.

Nurse, 2nd Lieutenant Margaret Masterton married her husband Flight Officer Rexford N.Manier, a glider pilot of the 47th Troop Carrier Squadron at St. Wulstans Church in Malvern at 3.15p.m. on 7th July 1944. The romance had begun in America when the couple had both been stationed at Army Air Base Laurinberg-Maxton, North Carolina.

Rexford Manier had enlisted in the Army Air Corps in Michigan November 1941, just prior to America's entry into the war. From here he was sent to Glider School in Elmira, New York. He became a Glider Pilot instructor in June 1942 and was promoted to Flight Officer. He was then transferred to Laurinberg-Maxton. Margaret Masterton arrived at the airbase on March 23rd

Margaret Masterton and Rexford Manier (M. Reeves).

1943; three days after Rexford had been admitted to the base hospital. On 28th March the couple were engaged to marry.

In May, Rexford was given orders to report to the Port of Embarkation to travel overseas to fly gliders in North Africa and in October he was transferred to Trapini, Sicily. In February 1944 Rexford was sent to England with the 47th Troop Carrier Squadron in readiness for the invasion of France.

Meanwhile in October 1943 Margaret had been assigned to the AAF School of Air Evacuation, Bowman Field, Kentucky and from here she was transferred to the Medical Department, Alliance Army Air Base on 1st November 1943. In January 1944 she was assigned to the 55th General Hospital and she arrived in England in March. In April the couple applied for permission to get married. Officially there should have been a delay of two months before permission was granted but Rexford applied for a waiver as the couple had already been engaged for a year.

Margaret had the honour of being the first to take part in a scheme instigated by Eleanor Roosevelt which the American Red Cross were running to provide wedding dresses for American service women. American brides were encouraged

```
                        47TH TROOP CARRIER SQUADRON
                        313TH TROOP CARRIER GROUP
                           APO #133, U. S. ARMY


                                                        1 April 1944




     SUBJECT:  Request for Permission to Marry.

        TO    :  Commanding General, 52nd Troop Carrier Wing, APO #638,
                  U. . Army  (Through Channels)


             1.  In accordance with provisions of ETOUSA Circular 88,
     3 November 1943 as amended by Circular 94, 1 December 1943, subject:
     Marriage, I hereby respectfully request permission to marry Lt.
     Margaret E. Masterson, N-787233, 55th General Hospital, APO #137,
     U. . Army.


                                          REXFORD N. MANIER
                                          Flt/O., Air Corps
                                          T-60385
       3 Incls:
       Incl - 1 - Acquiescence by Lt. Masterson.
       Incl - 2 - Request for Waiver.
       Incl - 3 - Certificate of Records.
     201 - Manier, R.N. (F/O)        1st Ind.              PWS/jda

     Hq. 47th T.C.Sqdn., 313th T.C.Gp., APO #133, U.S.Army, 3 April 1944.

     TO:  Commanding Officer, 313th T.C.Gp., APO #133, U.S.Army.

          1.  Approved.

          2.  F/O Manier has been made familiar with the various regulations
     and Theatre directives pertaining to marriage within the service.


                                          PAUL W. STEPHENS
                                          Major, Air Corps
                                          Commanding
     3 Incl;  n/c
```

Marriage request (M. Reeves).

154

```
                    47TH TROOP CARRIER SQUADRON
                    313TH TROOP CARRIER GROUP
                    APO #133, U. S. ARMY


                                            1 April 1944


SUBJECT:  Request for Waiver.

D       :  Commanding General, 52nd Troop Carrier Wing, APO #638,
           U.S. Army.  (Through Channels)

      1.  Reference is made to existing regulations, requiring a
lapse of two months waiting period for permission to marry.

      2.  I have been engaged to Lt. Masterson since 28 March 1943.
The last ten months were spent overseas.

      3.  At the present we are stationed near enough to become married
with proper authority.

      4.  Request the two month waiting period be waived because of
possible reseparation in the near future.


                                    REXFORD N. MANIER
                                    F1t/O., Air Corps
                                    T-60385
```

Request for waiver of waiting period to marry (M. Reeves).

to send their wedding dresses to the American Red Cross so that they could be worn by American service women in Britain who could not obtain wedding dresses because of war time shortages. The Red Cross was also able to supply Margaret with shoes to match the dress. After the wedding Margaret wrote to Eleanor Roosevelt to tell her about the wedding and she received a reply from the first lady.

Rexford Manier and his party were flown to the wedding by C47 which was piloted by 2nd Lt. Stanley Engle and co-piloted by 1st Lt. Gene Miller. Others in the party were 1st Lt. Richard P. Sarret, 2nd Lt. Louis C. Wood, Flight Officer

AMERICAN RED CROSS
APO.887.

June 26, 1944.

Lieutenant Margaret Masterson,
55th General Hospital,
APO.121.
U.S.Army.

Dear Miss Masterson,

We are sending you herewith, the wedding dress which seemed best to fit your requirements according to the measurements you gave me over the telephone.

We hope so much that you will enjoy wearing it and we must ask that no alterations be made and that you take as good care of it as possible so that someone else may have equal pleasure in wearing it at their wedding. Will you kindly see that it is returned to us immediately after the wedding, by registered post, unless you can find someone who will be coming to London in the immediate future.

Will you please see that a copy of your picture is sent us for our files as we shall be very much interested in seeing how you looked in the dress.

If you are in need of white satin slippers, would you please call me and let me know the size,because three pairs were sent with the dresses and possibly there might be one pair which would fit you.

Letter from Red Cross concerning wedding dress. (M. Reeves).

Charles W. Dorney Jr, Flight Officer Jack L. Flateau and Flight Officer Paul H. Huxhold. This was the first overseas wedding for a member of the 47th Troop Carrier Squadron. 1st Lieutenant Vifquain, the chaplain attached to the 55th, pronounced the vows for the couple. Flight Officer, Elwin E. Anderson, also a Glider pilot was the best man while the bridesmaid was 2nd Lieutenant Barbara Pailen, another nurse from the 55th General Hospital.

The wedding reception was held at the Westminster Hotel, Malvern Wells, where the dance band from the 55th played. The wedding cake was prepared by one of the cooks at the hospital. The couple spent a brief honeymoon in Birmingham before returning to their respective stations. Rexford was later

Top left: 1st Lt. Vifquain pronouncing vows for 2nd Lieutenant Margaret E. Masterton and Flight Officer Rexford N. Manier. (M. Reeves). Top right: Nurses of the 55th awaiting arrival of bride. (M. Reeves). Middle left and right: The happy couple outside St. Wulstan's Church. Bottom left: Wedding cake. Bottom right: Rexford and Margaret cutting the wedding cake baked by cooks from 55th General Hospital (M. Reeves).

WESTMINSTER ARMS HOTEL,

WEST MALVERN.

TELEGRAMS:
WESTMINSTER, WEST MALVERN

TELEPHONE No. 189

E. H. Shephard, *Proprietor.*

Room No....**14**.......

19 July 7ᵗ 8ᵗ	£ s. d.	£ s. d.	£ s. d.	£ s. d.	£ s. d.	£ s. d.	£ s. d.	TOTAL £ s. d.
Balance forward		1 56						
En Pension ...								
Apartments ...	1 1 .							
Breakfast ...		8 .						
Luncheons								
Teas ...								
Dinners								
Coffee ...								
Suppers								
Fruit, etc.								
Chocolates								
Visitors' S								
Ale ...								
Minerals								
Wines ...								
Spirits								
Cigarettes, etc.								
Fires								
Baths								
Newspapers ...								
Laundry ...								
Telephones ...								
Garage								
Car Hire ...								
Petrol								
Sundries ...								
TOTAL	1 56	2 26						£ 2 26

The receipt overlaid:

July 8 1944

RECEIVED from No. 14

the Sum of Two Pounds Two Shillings and Six Pence

WITH THANKS

R9

£ 2-2-6

Receipt from Westminster Arms Hotel for wedding reception (M. Reeves).

Left: Margaret Masterton in her Air Nurse summer uniform. (M. Reeves).
Right top: Letter sent by Chaplain Vifquain. (Authors' collection).
Right Bottom: Wedding reception at the Westminster Arms Hotel (M. Reeves).

awarded the Air Medal for his involvement in Operation Market Garden and was promoted to 2nd Lieutenant on October 17th 1944.

G.I. Ray Peterson, who met his wife in Malvern, was originally a patient at the 55th General Hospital. When the attack of Pearl Harbour occurred in December 1941 Ray was working as a Civil Servant at the Naval Air Station at Norfolk Virginia. He remembers clearly that weekend. All was quiet at the air station when he heard the teletype printer start working. It was bringing news of the attack. Ray could have remained working at the Naval Station as it was a reserved occupation but he wanted to join the army so when his draft papers came through he enlisted and took and passed exams for Officer Training.

He was put into the Army Specialist Training programme where he underwent training to prepare him for serving with the Occupying Forces at the end of the war. Unfortunately due to the high amount of casualties in the North Africa campaign the programme was cut short and Ray was sent for Basic Infantry Training.

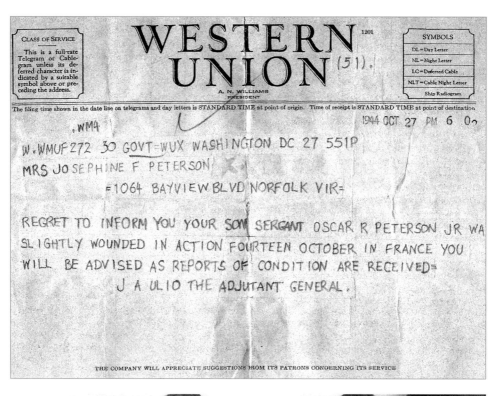

CLASS OF SERVICE

This is a full-rate Telegram or Cablegram unless its deferred character is indicated by a suitable symbol above or preceding the address.

WESTERN UNION (51).

A. N. WILLIAMS
PRESIDENT

SYMBOLS

DL = Day Letter
NL = Night Letter
LC = Deferred Cable
NLT = Cable Night Letter
Ship Radiogram

The filing time shown in the date line on telegrams and day letters is STANDARD TIME at point of origin. Time of receipt is STANDARD TIME at point of destination

. WM4

W . WMUF 272 30 GOVT=WUX WASHINGTON DC 27 551P

MRS JOSEPHINE F PETERSON

=1064 BAYVIEW BLVD NORFOLK VIR=

1944 OCT 27 PM 6 0o

REGRET TO INFORM YOU YOUR SON SERGANT OSCAR R PETERSON JR WA
SLIGHTLY WOUNDED IN ACTION FOURTEEN OCTOBER IN FRANCE YOU
WILL BE ADVISED AS REPORTS OF CONDITION ARE RECEIVED=
J A ULIO THE ADJUTANT GENERAL.

THE COMPANY WILL APPRECIATE SUGGESTIONS FROM ITS PATRONS CONCERNING ITS SERVICE

Top: Telegram informing Ray's parents of his injury in France (R. Peterson).
Bottom: Ray and Gloria (R. Peterson).

He remembers sailing on the Queen Mary to Scotland as part of the 50th Infantry Division. As he walked up the gangplank the men were given either a pink or a blue card. One colour signified sleeping on deck and one signified sleeping in a berth. Ray started the crossing in a berth but the crossing was so rough that he swapped his card so that he could sleep on deck. He arrived in the U.K. in June 1944.

From Scotland he travelled to the South coast by train and the sailed to France where he landed on Omaha Beach on D-Day +20. He was wounded in December 1944 in Metz. His unit had been pinned down in foxholes so at night he crept out to get fresh supplies. Unfortunately he was seen and the Germans threw a trench mortar at him. Ray heard it coming but could not avoid it so he was wounded in the leg. He was taken to a field hospital where he awaited transportation to take him back to England. The following night two medics arrived with a stretcher to carry him to the ambulance. Ray took one look at them and decided they wouldn't be able to carry him so he suggested that he hop to the ambulance. He was flown back to Southampton and from there took the train to Malvern and a short ambulance ride to Wood Farm.

While at the hospital he and one of the other patients who had been wounded in the arm and wore a sling decided to visit the local pub. In hospital issue dressing gown and slippers the two made their way up the hill to the Hornyold Arms. As they opened the door, to their dismay, they saw that the pub was filled with high ranking officers from the hospital whose first reaction was '*What an earth are you doing here?*' and second was '*What would you like to drink?*'

After three months of physiotherapy the doctors decided that because of his injuries he would never be fit for active service so they planned to send him back to the U.S. Ray requested permission to stay at the 55th and was given a job at the Dental Section Reception until the 55th left in June 1945.

Ray met his future wife, Gloria, at a dance in the Winter Gardens in Malvern. He attended the dance with colleagues from the base and remembers seeing three attractive girls sitting near the Orchestra, a blonde, a brunette and a redhead. One of his friends who knew the girls introduced him to them. A romance blossomed between Ray and the brunette and towards the end of the war they got married.

Eventually Ray travelled back to the U.S. and returned to his job which involved travelling around the country. While travelling towards New Mexico he phoned home and was told that his wife had arrived by ship in New York but was not allowed to leave the ship until a family member came to collect her. Fortunately Ray had a cousin living in New York who was able to collect Gloria from the boat. Ray was finally reunited with his wife and after a few years they decided to settle down and bring up their family in England.

Local girl, Brenda Bridges also had hopes of marrying a medic from the 55th General Hospital. Brenda had met Jim Abe Jenkins at the Reindeer Pub in Worcester (now an arcade) while they were both with groups of friends. They started seeing each other and Jim was introduced to the family. He would often visit the family at Brenda's Gran's house, sometimes bringing tins of fruit.

When Brenda became pregnant a social worker visited Colonel Gill to see what arrangements could be made. However Jim denied that he knew Brenda. Shortly after this he was sent to serve as a medic in Germany. Brenda tried to get in touch with Jim several times to inform him of the birth of his daughter but she was never successful.

In 2002 Brenda's grandson, Steve Mezzone, took up the search. On the same day in July 2007 he received two emails concerning his grandfather. One was to say that the authorities of a crematory in Gurdon, Arkansas had

Left: Brenda Bridges. Right: Jim Abe Jenkins (G. Brown).

located the grave and the second, arriving 20 minutes later, was from the Arkansas Democrat Gazette to inform him that they had located some of his grandfather's relatives.

Unfortunately Jim died in 1984 and by this time Brenda had also died but Brenda's daughter, Glennis and grandson, Steve travelled to visit the grave and meet the surviving relatives of Jim, who had never had any other children even though he had been married twice. After the war he had joined the Merchant Marine and travelled the world, only returning home from time to time. When the family met Glennis they could see the family likeness immediately.

Chapter 19

TOP KNOTCH JOB

A s the 55th made plans to return home from France in August 1945 they decided to produce a book: " ... *as a memento of all of its overseas members" (55th General Hospital Archives)*.

By the end of September the manuscript was complete, telling the story of the 55th since its inception at Camp Robinson and ending with its work at Mourmelon in France. The manuscript also included drawings:

" ... *to refresh our memories of moonlit marches, retreat ceremonies and other things" (55th General Hospital Archives)*.

The manuscript was taken to the authorities for official approval which it received, but the approval was conditional on funding at individual or private expense. By this time only a handful of the original enlisted men and none of the officers remained as most of the original members had been rotated back to the States by this time, their places being taken by replacements. As Colonel Gill wrote:

" ... *the strangers who bore our name were not interested in helping with the booklet" (55th General Hospital Archives)*.

The manuscript was filed away and, to our knowledge, remains unprinted apart from the roster of personnel which was copied and distributed.

As the Colonel looked through the list of men and women he had served with he mused about how fortunate the personnel of the 55th had been:

"We really suffered very little; we were well clothed, warm and well fed" (55th General Hospital Archives).

He recalled that it was necessary for a small number who served with the unit to return to the United States because of illness, also a number of the corpsmen had

Nurses in Battle Togs Embark for France

LONDON, June 9 (UP).—A party of American Nurses, en route to France, embarked from a coast town aboard a transport yesterday. The nurses wore battle blouses, breeches and gaiters and marched aboard carrying duffle bags.

Press cutting describing movement of 55th General Hospital nurses to France.

Margaret Masterton (M. Reeves).

been transferred to combat units during the latter stages of the Battle of the Bulge when replacements were needed. He mentions a group of nine drivers who were transferred to combat duties. Five of these were killed in action. He concludes:

"As each reads the roster let it recall many most pleasant memories of great experience. We did a top knotch job in the care of the sick, we maintained a fine relationship with higher headquarters and we made a substantial contribution to Anglo-American relations in England. We have a right to be proud of our accomplishments. We served our country well in war and we will serve it well in peace" (55th General Hospital Archives).

Chapter 20

CONCLUSION

As the American personnel left Malvern the hospital sites took on new roles. Wood Farm was occupied by Dutch men and women of the armed forces and nursing services as soon as it became vacant. The site was also used as a transit camp for Dutch civilians en route from Holland to the liberated colonies in Africa. Many of the personnel had been transferred to Wood Farm from a camp near Wolverhampton.

The new Commanding Officer for the camp was Colonel Andre de la Porte although Mager G.W. Tvon Walraven temporarily took command for the first few months. He had been recalled to Holland from the colonies in 1939 as he was a military engineer. He had been imprisoned by the Germans for 18 months but escaped to join the Dutch Underground Movement.

Later the camp was used for displaced persons from Latvia, Lithuania, Estonia and the Ukraine. When it was no longer needed for housing troops it reverted back to its original use as part of the Worcestershire Golf Course.

Hut base at Wood Farm c.2009 (M. Collins).

Top and bottom left: Buildings originally built for the 55th General Hospital still standing c.2009. (M. Collins). Right: Merebrook Camp when being used by the REME in the 1950's (J. Geeves).

Merebrook was used by the Royal Engineers from 1946 until 1958. The S.A.S. (Special Air Service) was based there for a few months in 1959. When the British Forces left the site most of the wartime buildings were demolished by Worcestershire County Council, a handful were left for industrial use. The Officers' Mess is being used for a riding school.

Brickbarns was used by the British Army as a training site when the American Forces left in December 1945. In the 1950's it was acquired by the Ministry of Health for use as a Tuberculosis Hospital although it was necessary to make a

*Main Gate at Merebrook while the camp was being used
by the R.E.M.E. (J. Foster).*

Riding School, formerly the Officer's Mess, Merebrook (M. Collins).

number of alterations to the site first. Between 1945 and 1960 new antibiotics were discovered to treat T.B. and by the 1960's the disease was under control. Fewer beds were needed for T.B. patients and many sanatoriums closed down.

In the early 1970's the hospital became a 350 bed psychiatric hospital for the West Midlands Health Authority. Its methods were seen as unique as it aimed to rehabilitate patients back into the community at a time when most patients resided in long stay wards in large asylums. Moves were made to close the hospital as early as 1977. It eventually closed at the end of 1986

Top: Aerial view of St. Wulstan's Hospital in the 1980's showing that many of the original buildings built for the 56th General Hospital were still standing and being used. (Judges). Bottom left: World War II U.S. Army Dodge Ambulance outside buildings at Merebrook (M. Collins). Right: Formerly the Supply Building at Merebrook (M. Collins).

despite passionate opposition to the closure by many of those involved with the hospital.

Planning permission was granted for St. Wulstans Housing Estate on the site on the condition that 55 acres of land were handed over to the district council to be made into a Nature Reserve. In 1994 the hospital buildings

THIS MEMORIAL ERECTED BY
THE PEOPLE OF MALVERN,
COMMEMORATES SEVEN
AMERICAN GENERAL HOSPITALS
WITH TEN THOUSAND BEDS,
AND THE 12TH. GENERAL
HOSPITAL CENTER, SITUATED
NEAR MALVERN 1943 - 1945
DURING THE WORLD WAR

*Plaque now to be found in Malvern Museum along with
a display of photos from the hospitals. (M.Collins).*

were demolished and saplings and wild flowers planted. The Nature Reserve was officially opened in 1997.

In January 1950 a fund was launched to provide a plaque commemorating the role of the American hospitals in the Malvern area. A public meeting was held and a vote was taken as to where it should be placed. For the Malvern Gazette the move was 'long overdue' and it wanted to see more done to commemorate the part played in the war of the various military units in Malvern.

"We still think the council, as the town's officially elected body should devise some project whereby in one central place visitors and residents in many years to come may see a chronological record of the way that Malvern once became a haven and a training ground for the forces of freedom … a plaque, while welcome, would never sum up the happy memories of the American occupation." (Malvern Gazette).

Appendix 1

ABBREVIATIONS

A.A. Anti Aircraft
A.E.F. Allied Expeditionary Force
A.F.D. Assistant Field Director (Leader of the Red Cross at a base)
A.R.C. American Red Cross
AWOL Absent Without Leave

B.P.O. Base Post Office

C.O. Commanding Officer
C.P.R. Cardio-Pulmonary Resuscitation
Col. Colonel
Comm. Z. Communication Zone – area behind the combat zone i.e. U.K.
Cpl. Corporal

D.E. Destroyer Escort

E.T.O. European Theatre of Operations

G.W.R. Great Western Railway

H.Q. Headquarters

K.P. Kitchen Police – (duties in the kitchen)

L.M.S. London, Midland, Scotland Railway
L.S.T. Landing Ship Tank
Lt. Lieutenant

M.C. Master of Ceremonies
M.P. Military Police
Maj. Major

N.P. Neuro Psychiatric
N.C.O. Non-Commissioned Officer

O.D. Olive Drab, referring to military colour of khaki
O.R. Operating Room

P.O.W. Prisoner of War
P.T.O. Pacific Theatre of Operations
Pfc Private First Class
Pvt. Private
P.X. Post Exchange – U.S. equivalent of NAAFI

R.A.F. Royal Air Force
R.A.A.F Royal Australian Air Force

Sgt. Sergeant

T/E Table of Equipment
T/O Table of Organization
Tec.4 Technician 4th Grade

W.A.C. Women's Army Corps
W.V.S. Women's Voluntary Service – British civilian voluntary organisation

Z.I. Zone of the Interior (U.S.)

GLOSSARY

Ambulatory – patients able to walk

Assigned – having permanent duties at a base

Limited Assignment – having temporary duties at a base

Litter – stretcher

Closed Wards – hospital wards where patients are restricted to the ward

Open Wards – hospital wards where patients are not restricted to the ward

Convalescent Hospitals – (C.H.) – Treated convalescing troops sent from station or general hospitals

General Hospital – (G.H.) – Hospitals with 1082 beds (although at times when the need arose this number was larger). Mainly intended for soldiers wounded during combat

Station Hospitals – (S.H.) – Hospitals with 834 beds serving the needs of troops in training. Often attached to a base.

Operation Overlord – Codename for Allied invasion of France

Operation Bolero – Codename for the build up of troops in Britain in readiness for D-Day

Mess hall – dining room

Motor Pool – Unit that repaired and maintained the vehicles attached to a unit

Replacement Depot – Transit camp for personnel awaiting assignment.

Special Service – Education and Entertainment section responsible for the morale of troops on a base

St. Dunstans – Charity for the blind servicemen

Western Base Section – Western quarter of U.K.

AMERICAN MILITARY UNITS KNOWN TO BE IN MALVERN 1943-45

Blackmore Park – Plant 4172 and Plant 4173
> 701st Medical Sanitation Co. – March 1944
> 19th General Hospital Medical Detachment – Sep 1943 – May 1944
> 19th General Hospital Detachment of Patients – Sep 1943 – May 1944
> 769th Military Police Battalion (ZI) Company A, Detachment A
> 137th Army Postal Unit
> 93rd General Hospital – May 1944 – Sep. 1945
> Detachment of Patients 4172 Hospital Plant
> Detachment of Patients 4173 Hospital Plant
> 90th General Hospital – Feb 1944 – July 1944
> 65th General Hospital – Oct 1943 – May 1944
> 155th General Hospital – July 1944 – July 1945
> 255th Medical Detachment
> 256th Medical Detachment
> 374th M.P. Patrol Unit
> 114th Army Postal Unit Type A
> 115th Army Postal Unit Type A
> 3960th Signal Switchboard Detachment

Merebrook – Plant 4175
> 53rd General Hospital HQ – Mar 1944 – Aug 1945
> 53rd General Hospital Medical Detachment
> Detachment of Patients 4175 Hospital Plant

Wood Farm – Plant 4176
> 55th General Hospital – Mar 1944 – June 1945
> Detachment of Patients 4176 Hospital Plant

Brickbarns – Plant 4174
56th General Hospital – Nov 1943 – Jan 1944
96th General Hospital – Jan 1944 – July 1945
312th Station Hospital – July 1945 – Aug 1945
53rd General Hospital – Aug 1945 – Sep 1945
231st Station Hospital – Sep 1945 – Dec 1945
Detachment of Patients Hospital Plant 4174

Malvern Link
5th Hospital Train Unit
12th Medical Hospital Centre
66th Army Postal Unit
106th Finance Distribution Unit
121st Army Postal Unit

Appendix 4

ARMY HOSPITAL CENTERS

Hospital Center	Hospital Group	Place	Date of Activation
12	5	Malvern	April 1944
15	4	Cirencester	April 1944
801	1	Taunton	Feb. 1945
802	2	Blandford	Feb. 1945
803	3	Devizes	Feb. 1945
804	6	Whitchurch	Feb. 1945
(Originally 6801 provisional-activated June 1944)			
805	7	Newmarket	Feb. 1945

N.B. Hospital Groups designated October 1944

Map showing Medical Centers in the U.K. (U.S. Military archives).

Appendix 5

U.S. ARMY HOSPITALS IN U.K. 1944

Plant No.	Site	Hospitals Unit
4100	Truro	314SH
4101	Tavistock	115SH
4102	Moretonhampstead	?
4103	Newton Abbot	124GH
4104	Exeter	36SH
4105	Barnstaple	313SH
4106	Bishops Lydeard	185GH
4107	Norton Manor	101GH
4108	Taunton	67GH
4109	Axminster	315SH
4110	Yeovil, Houndstone	169GH
4111	Yeovil, Lufton	121GH
4112	Sherborne	228SH
4113	Frome St. Quintin	305SH
4114	Blandford	22GH
4115	Blandford	119GH
4116	Blandford	125GH
4117	Blandford	131GH
4118	Blandford	140GH
4119	Wimborne	106GH
4120	Ringwood	104GH
4121	Netley	110SH
4122	Winchester	38SH
4123	Stockbridge	34GH
4124	Odstock	158GH
4125	Grimsdith	250SH
4126	Warminster	216GH
4127	Tidworth	3SH
4128	Perham Downs	103GH
4129	Everleigh	187GH

4130	Devizes	141GH
4131	Devizes	128GB
4132	Erlestoke Park	102GH
4133	Bath	160SH
4134	Falfield	94GH
4135	Malmesbury	120SH
4136	Lydiard Park	302SH
4137	Swindon	154GH
4138	Chiseldon	130SH
4139	Marlborough	347SH
4140	Hermitage	98GH
4141	Checkendon	306GH
4142	Kingwood	304GH
4143	Wheatley	97GH
4144	Headington	91GH
4145	Middleton Stoney	318SH
4146	Ramsden	317SH
4147	Burford	61GH
4148	Fairford	186GH
4149	Cirencester	188GH
4150	Cirencester	192GH
4151	Daglingworth	111GH
4152	Stowell Park	160GH
4153	Ullenwood	110GH
4154	Blockley	327SH
4155	Moreton	–
4156	Fairford	–
4157	Salisbury	152SH
4165	Tyntesfield	74GH
4166	Bristol	117GH
4167	Stoneleigh	307SH
4168	Bromsgrove	123SH
4169	Wolverley	52GH
4170	Bewdley	297GH
4171	Bewdley	114GH
4172	Blackmore Park	93GH
4173	Blackmore Park	155GH
4174	Malvern Wells	96GH
4175	Malvern Wells	53GH

4176	Malvern Wells	55GH
4177	Leominster	135GH
4178	Foxley	123GH
4179	Foxley	156GH
4180	Kington	122GH
4181	Kington	107GH
4182	Abergavenny	279SH
4183	Rhyd Lafar	81GH
4184	Carmarthen	232SH
4185	Lichfleld	33SH
4186	Shugborough	312SH
4187	Sudbury Derby	182GH
4188	Whittington	68GH
4189	Oteley Deer Park	137GH
4190	Overton	83GH
4191	Penley	129GH
4192	Iscoyd Park	82GH
4193	Saighton	109GH
4194	Clatterbridge	157GH
4195	Stockton Heath	168SH
4196	Davey Hulme	10SH
4197	Glasgow	316SH
4198	Harrogate	115GH
4199	Harrogate	116GH
4200	Mansfield	184GH
4201	Nocton Hall	7GH
4202	Allington	348SH
4203	Thorpe North	303SH
4204	Diddington	49SH
4205	Cambridge	163GH
4206	Newport	280SH
4207	Braintree	121SH
4208	Acton, Suffolk	136SH
4209	Redgrave Park	65GH
4210	Wymondham	231SH
4211	North Mimms	1GH
4212	–	–
4213	Packington	77SH
4261	London	16SH

ACKNOWLEDGEMENTS

Brickbarns Farm
Ed Black, Stephen Gill, Richard Lloyd, H.E. Harvey, John Shook, John Spalding, Jackie Styles, R.Waters, Browen Williams.

Merebrook
Roger Bovee, Judy Brinkman, Joe Foster, Bob Garrison, J.C. Geeves, Jan Green, Ruby Johnson, Al Lombino, Maggie Poe, Marva Stateler, Arnold Wallace, Phil Williams, Rosemary Williams, Peggy Webb.

Wood Farm
Glennis Brown, Terry Cole, John Cramer, Malcolm Mason, Basil Moss, Ray Peterson, Michele Reeves, Mr Sanders, Heather Talbot.

Other Contributors
Tony Allison, John Bowen, Mike Boyce, Gerald Buttock, Irene Carpenter, Linda Conn (Cary Area Public Library, Illinois), Pete Evans, R.Gardner (U.S. National Library of Medicine) Marge Hawker, Gill Holt, Brian Iles, Ray Kinsey, Peter Lewis, Dorothy Parkes, Robert Rotundo, Charlie Williams, Godfrey Williams.

Publications and Organisations
National Archives and Records Administration:
    53rd General Hospital and A.R.C.
    55th General Hospital and A.R.C.
    96th General Hospital and A.R.C.
    56th General Hospital
    56th General Hospital Nurses Archives
    231st Station Hospital A.R.C.
    53rd General Hospital Year Book
    96th General Hospital Year Book
    American Legion

Army Times
Bulge Bugle
National Amvet
Order of the Purple Heart
Retired Officer Magazine
Shaef Communique
Stars and Stripes
V.F.W. Magazine
The History of Neuroscience in Autobiography – Larry R.Squire
The Ninety Sixth General Hospital – The Story of an Army
Neuropsychiatric Hospital – Henry Myers.
Malvern Gazette
Malvern Library
Malvern Tourist Information Centre

BY THE SAME AUTHOR

Letters for Victory, Brewin Books, 1993.
Somewhere in the Midlands, Brewin Books, 1998.
They Also Serve, Brewin Books, 2001.
Camp Foxley, Brewin Books, 2005.
Blackmore Park in World War II, Brewin Books, 2008.